Local Affairs

A Play

Richard Harris

A SAMUEL FRENCH ACTING EDITION

SAMUEL
FRENCH
FOUNDED 1830

SAMUELFRENCH-LONDON.CO.UK
SAMUELFRENCH.COM

ISBN 978-0-573-11236-2

www.samuelfrench-london.co.uk

www.samuelfrench.com

FOR AMATEUR PRODUCTION ENQUIRIES

UNITED KINGDOM AND WORLD EXCLUDING NORTH AMERICA

plays@SamuelFrench-London.co.uk

020 7255 4302/01

Each title is subject to availability from Samuel French,

depending upon country of performance.

LOCAL AFFAIRS

Presented on tour by Bill Kenwright with the following cast of characters:

Norma	Adrienne Corri
Mrs Hinson	Irene Handl
Charles	Ronald Hewlett
Susan	Cheryl Hall
David	Mark Eden
Keith	Christopher Beeny
Hilary	Hilary Crane
Peter	Michael Knowles
Katy	Kirsten Cooke

The play directed by Terence Frisby

The action of the play takes place in the living-room, bedroom and kitchen of three different houses

ACT I   Afternoon to early evening
ACT II   Immediately following

Time—the present

ACT I

A living-room, a bedroom, a kitchen. Saturday, early afternoon

The rooms represent a house on a new and "superior" twelve-unit development. They also represent three houses on the same development. We should be much aware of this newness—and even more, of the architect's blinkered vision—so that what we are perhaps presented with is more of the drawing-board than of the home

The living-room occupies the largest area. In it are a television, two polished hardwood cabinets, a sofa, a coffee-table and a non-matching easy chair. All the cushions are plumped and immaculate. There is a door C in the rear wall, above which is a long, diagonal and prominent crack in the plaster. R of the living-room is the bedroom, which could be slightly raised. There is a double bed with a low headboard unit, to one side of which is a built-in dressing-table and wardrobes unit. Upstage of this is a door leading into the en suite bathroom. A second door in the rear wall leads out on to a landing. The windows to the bedroom and living-room are in the "fourth wall". L of the living-room is the kitchen. There are a table and chairs, a fridge, a sink unit with cupboards underneath, and counter units with cupboards above them. A door DL leads directly through into the garage. Upstage of this door, above the sink unit, a window gives a glimpse over the new wooden fence of the other houses. There is a door in the rear wall leading to the hall. The furnishings in the rooms are by no means final and include both new items and those brought from previous homes. There should be no personal effects showing. There might be an unpacked tea-chest in the bedroom or glimpsed on the landing

When the CURTAIN *rises, the living-room and the kitchen are in daylight but the bedroom has the "curtains" drawn. We can make out the figure of someone (Susan) asleep in the bed. In the kitchen, Norma is sitting at the (new) table, consulting her beloved notepad. She is in her mid-forties, short and a little on the plump side. On the table are a pencil, a steel tape measure, her handbag and car keys. Mrs Hinson is in the living-room. She is a working-class widow in her late sixties. Her mind is a mixture of pure gristle and animal cunning. Going a bit deaf, and more so if it suits her. She dresses, tip to toe, from Marks and Sparks, and is wearing a floral pinnie and slippers. She is bashing around with a vacuum cleaner which she leaves running as she dabs with her duster at a mark she has just noticed on one of the polished wood cabinets. As she does so, Norma gets up and starts measuring a length of counter top, with the tape*

Mrs Hinson realizes she will need something more to shift the mark. She switches off the vacuum cleaner and exits as:

Charles enters the kitchen from the hall. He is forty-five, a doctor. Solidly built, has a moustache. He's wearing his favourite weekend cardigan and is very intent on something that has been exercising his mind all morning. He watches Norma for a moment

Charles The thing is—fancy dress—you want something simple—right?
Norma We can't have a deep freeze.
Charles Now then—why can't we?
Norma Because it won't fit.
Charles You wouldn't want it in here anyway.
Norma Well where would I want it?
Charles (*indicating*) In the garage.

Norma regards the garage door and considers a moment

Norma You're absolutely right, of course you are, clever old you. (*She ticks off her notes*) Now then, dishwasher.
Charles Norma, I'm trying to talk to you about this stupid party.
Norma Sorry, darling. Yes?
Charles Fancy dress—no point going mad—something simple—right?
Norma Right. (*She puts the pad, pencil and tape into her handbag*)
Charles Because I think I've got an idea.
Norma Good. (*She takes up her bag and keys*) I'm just popping across to the gardening centre.
Charles (*grittily*) I see.
Norma I'm sure it's a very good idea but we'll talk about it later. (*She stops at the garage door*) Oh yes—have you spoken to that man who's going to do the wallpaper?
Charles What? No.
Norma Because I was speaking to Mr Thingy—you know, at the clinic—and he said with a new house we should leave it at least another month.
Charles (*flatly*) Did he.
Norma Don't—worry.

Norma exits into the garage

Charles stands for a moment, glowering, and then exits after Norma as:

Mrs Hinson enters the living-room with the dampened duster which she uses on the mark as:

In the bedroom, Susan, suddenly awake, sits up in the bed, realizing that she is alone. She switches on the bedside light

Susan Keith?

She gets out of bed and moves to peer from the drawn "curtains". She is in her late twenties, wears unflattering pyjamas, is overweight and aware of it, tense and trying not to be. She lets the "curtain" drop, sighs and looks somewhat disconsolately around the room

She exits into the bathroom as:

Mrs Hinson switches on the vacuum cleaner and resumes her bashing around

David enters the living-room. He's forty and her only son. As his mother would say, he's done all right for himself. She's the root of all his problems: guilt is his second name. He is wearing glasses, lightweight grey trousers and a golf sweater and is carrying a potted plant arrangement with a ribbon tied around the bowl

On seeing his mother, he sighs and makes to say something but realizes she won't hear and puts down the bowl and switches off the cleaner at the wall. She turns to regard him, hand on hip, as he winds up the electric lead, moving towards her

David You've done it again, haven't you? Stop changing things *round*. (*He clips the flex on to the machine*) We like the chair where it *is*. (*He moves the chair from one side of the sofa to the other*)

Mrs Hinson Well in my opinion it looks better over there.

David And you've been polishing the front doorstep again, haven't you?

Mrs Hinson Well you're not saying there's anything wrong with that, are you?

David I nearly broke my neck just now . . .

Mrs Hinson Pass me my bag, will you? (*She tetchily indicates*)

David takes up her handbag and passes it to her as she sits on the sofa. Mrs Hinson delves into her bag for a bottle of pills, but does not quite get around to taking one

Turning the hoover off sudden like that, you've brought on one of my heads.

David I don't like you cleaning the step, I don't like seeing you on your hands and knees, I never have done.

Mrs Hinson All I am trying to do, migraine or no migraine, is clean this place up before Madam gets home.

David For which I am very grateful . . . oh yes . . . (*He takes up the bowl*) . . . I brought you a little present. (*He bends to kiss her cheek, holding the bowl for her*) Thanks.

Mrs Hinson What's this for?

David For . . . looking after me.

Mrs Hinson It'll only die. You shouldn't waste your money, you've got enough on your plate.

David That's what I like about you, Mum.

Mrs Hinson You know what I mean.

David Yes I know what you mean. (*He again kisses her briefly—kissing never did come very easily in their family—and behind her back practises the little chip shots that let him down so badly in his game of golf that morning*) What I'm trying to say is—you've been here five days and you haven't stopped cleaning.

Mrs Hinson Well I had to, didn't I, state the place was in. I mean, no disrespect son, but she's not exactly one for soap and water, is she?

David Yes, all right, Mum.

Mrs Hinson I could have grown radishes in the dust under this furniture. I shouldn't think it's been touched for a twelve-month.

David We've only been here four weeks and I think she's got it in pretty good order—which reminds me—please stop moving things around in the kitchen, please leave the cupboards as they are.

Mrs Hinson I can't *reach* anything.

David Then ask *me*.

Mrs Hinson You're never here. I mean, look at this morning, off you go without so much as a word. Where've you been, anyway? Playing golf, I suppose.

David Fat chance of that.

Mrs Hinson I thought Saturdays she let you play golf.

David There was a panic on in the office—I meant to leave you a note. (*He takes off his glasses to polish them with his handkerchief, inspecting the lenses myopically. He invariably does this when lying*)

Mrs Hinson Well you should have had a nice game, it would have done you good—all this running about, making decisions—and I don't suppose you've had a thing in your stomach all morning.

David Where've you put the paper?

Mrs Hinson I put the paper where the paper belongs. (*She lifts one of the sofa cushions and pulls out a copy of "The Guardian"*)

Mrs Hinson Why don't you get a decent paper?

David I'll be taking you *home* tomorrow.

Mrs Hinson You said you'd order one.

David (*patiently*) I'll get you one . . . when I do the shopping.

Mrs Hinson And the *TV Times*.

David And the *TV Times*, yes.

Mrs Hinson I mean, what sort of a house doesn't have the *TV Times*?

David (*glancing out of the "window"*) Hello . . . looks like they've got trouble with their plumbing already.

Mrs Hinson (*moving to stand next to him, nosily*) Who has?

David (*indicating*) Chap across the road. He's got himself a whatsit, a sink plunger.

Mrs Hinson Your father was wonderful with sinks. People used to send for him, you know, and him on the buses.

She moves away and flits around with her duster as David sits in the chair, opening the paper and gratefully stretching out weary legs

Mind you, they're very easy, these houses. Not like your last one. Now that was a lovely house that was. I felt very proud when I came to that house. When I was allowed to come to that house. Victorian, wasn't it?

David (*reading*) Yeah . . . Victorian damp, Victorian draughty . . .

Mrs Hinson These houses are all the same, I can't think why you moved. I suppose it was her idea.

David It was our idea and the name is Hilary.

Mrs Hinson Oh yes? (*She indicates*) When are you going to get this crack fixed?

David (*reading*) I've told you: the builders will do it.

Mrs Hinson Your poor dear father wouldn't have left it like this.

David No he wouldn't.

Mrs Hinson No he wouldn't—he would have filled it in even if it meant staying up all night.

David Especially if it meant staying up all night.

Mrs Hinson (*her deaf bit*) Pardon?

David (*folding away the paper*) Mum . . . these are new houses. You always get a bit of settlement in a new house. That's why you don't decorate straight away. It's nothing to worry about.

Mrs Hinson It would have worried your father.

The telephone rings off in the hall

(*Immediately, imperiously*) Phone!

David exits into the hallway to answer the phone, taking the newspaper with him and leaving the door slightly ajar

Mrs Hinson moves close to the door, trying to listen, but the door is pointedly pulled shut. Thwarted, she glares around, sees the chair and pulls it across, back to where she prefers it. It's an effort, but she's determined. At the same time:

Charles enters the kitchen from the hall, carrying a brand new sink plunger. He opens a drawer and sorts out a ball of string and a meat skewer which he tests to see if it will make a hole in the rubber on the plunger, as:

Susan enters the bedroom from the bathroom. She takes up her cigarettes and matches and moves to look down from the "window". Throughout the following dialogue, she gets back into bed and tries very hard not to light a cigarette

Charles exits from the kitchen to the hall with the plunger, string and skewer as:

David enters the living-room, without the newspaper and very preoccupied. He looks at his mother for a moment and then automatically returns the chair to its rightful position

David That was . . . er . . . that was the, er, hospital. (*He polishes his glasses*) Hilary that is. She's, er, she's seen the specialist and he says . . . she can come out any time she likes so she's . . . getting a car. She'll be here in half an hour.

Mrs Hinson Yes, well, you'll be pleased to have her home, won't you, son? I mean, she is your wife. (*She somehow makes that heavy with inference*)

David D'you know—I tell you she's in hospital and not once have you asked me how she is.

Mrs Hinson I don't have to—you tell me.

David Wouldn't it have been nice if you'd asked?

Mrs Hinson Well it can't be anything serious or they wouldn't be letting her out a day early, would they? I mean, I might not know much, but one thing you cannot fault me on is my intimate knowledge of the National Health Service. Besides, all I get from you is, she's being *inspected*.

David Examined.

Mrs Hinson Well, whatever it is. No wonder she can't get pregnant, all this poking about she authorizes.

David (*for the umpteenth time*) We do not—want—children—OK?

Mrs Hinson She's never *out* of hospital.

David (*holding up a finger*) Once. (*He makes it two fingers*) Twice.

Mrs Hinson What did she say when you told her I was staying here and looking after you?

David I shall have to take you home.

Mrs Hinson (*knowing full-well*) You haven't told her, have you? Well then, now we know where we stand.

David No I didn't tell her and I'm taking you home.

Mrs Hinson But I'm not packed or anything.

David I'll give you a hand. (*He slaps his hands together cheerfully*) Off we go then.

Mrs Hinson But you were taking me tomorrow *morning*.

David Yes and I'm very sorry . . .

Mrs Hinson That's right, turn against me.

David No-one is . . .

Mrs Hinson I knew we should never have sent you to that grammar school.

David Look. I've done it all wrong. I should have told her you were here. But you know what it's like, the pair of you.

Mrs Hinson (*doing her close to tears bit*) I don't want to be the cause of any trouble.

David You're not.

Mrs Hinson I've only ever wanted to be helpful.

David Yes I know you have.

Mrs Hinson Your Rosemary wouldn't have worried about my being here.

David I'm not married to Rosemary any more.

Mrs Hinson No you're not and more's the pity.

David Yes well we know all about that, don't we? (*He slaps his hands together, very positive*) I know what's right, I've made up my mind, I'm very sorry, no more arguing, off we go.

Mrs Hinson I don't like being rushed, I'm too old to be rushed, I'm your mother. (*She sniffs into her handkerchief*)

A moment

David You're absolutely right. You're here and that's an end to it. If you could just give me a minute with her to . . . square things up. Tell you what—we need a loaf—if you could—you know . . .

Mrs Hinson (*patting his hand*) Yes all right son, you're a good boy, I know you only ever try to do what's best.

David (*kissing her brow briefly*) I'll get your coat then, shall I?

Mrs Hinson Yes please son, it's in my room. (*She gets up, clutching at her handbag. Where she goes, the bag goes too*)

David exits

(*Calling after him*) I was going to make you a nice rice pudding. (*She turns and surveys the room distastefully*) Trust her to spoil it.

Under her breath, she mouths—silently but clearly—"The bitch", and exits from the living-room as:

In the bedroom, Susan takes out a cigarette and is about to light it as:

Keith enters the bedroom from the landing. He is wearing a scruffy dressing-gown and carries a tray with two mugs of tea. A newspaper is tucked under his arm. He's from Manchester and finds it very difficult to sit still for five minutes

Keith What's this then, you're awake.
Susan It's two o'clock in the afternoon.
Keith What did we say?
Susan We didn't say all *day*.
Keith I promised you tea in bed and tea in bed you shall have—come on, Sue, don't spoil it—and you don't need that thing for a start.

She looks at him for a moment, then smiles and abandons the cigarettes as he gets into bed beside her, putting the tray on his lap and passing her a mug. They both make a great effort to be bright

This is the life, eh?
Susan It's all right for a day or so, in fact it's very nice—but I don't think I could make a career out of it.
Keith Lying in bed? "Certain" women have done, you know. (*He waggles his eyebrows like Groucho*)

She makes to drink her tea, but pauses

Susan They'll be all right, won't they?

He's been waiting for it

Keith Course they will.
Susan It's just that . . . she's getting on. You know. She might think she can cope but—I mean—if anything should happen . . .
Keith Nothing's going to happen.
Susan I just wish we had the phone on.
Keith Well we haven't. She's their grannie. They'll be loving it, the lot of 'em and you know it.
Susan Tell me I'm being daft, go on.
Keith It's the first time they've been away, you're bound to feel strange. I do and I'm not with 'em all day.
Susan The house seems so quiet.
Keith You needed a rest and you're getting one—shut up and drink your tea.

She smiles at him. They sip their tea as:

Charles enters the kitchen from the hall, carrying the string and the skewer. He has a woman's scarf knotted on his head, a black eye-patch over one eye and the sink plunger tied to one of his knees with string. He returns the string and skewer to the drawer as:

Norma enters from the garage. She comes in backwards, keys between her teeth, handbag under her arm, and is carrying a miniature tree, staked, in a pot. She lovingly puts the tree on the table and admires it

Norma What do you think of this?

Charles What is it?

Norma It's a miniature willow. It's to go with the pond.

Charles Not that bloody pond again. Why do we have to have a pond?

Norma Don't raise your voice, they're very sensitive.

Charles I suppose you want me to introduce myself. (*To the tree*) Good afternoon, the name's Prentiss.

Norma I'd rather you didn't bother.

Charles Why? Does it only speak Japanese?

Norma No, because the last tree you spoke to suddenly lost the will to live. (*To the tree*) Who's a pretty boy then?

Charles Norma . . . what about *this*?

She looks at him. He strikes a pose, using the plunger as a wooden leg

Norma Is that the scarf I brought back from Paris?

Charles A *pirate*.

Norma Yes, darling but will you be wearing your cardigan or slipping into something a little more nautical?

Charles This is simply the general idea, yes or no?

Norma Yes I'm sure it's very nice. (*Indicating the plunger*) What's that thing?

Charles Obviously it's my wooden leg.

Norma Yes I know that darling, but do you intend hopping about on it all evening, bearing in mind how nasty your veins can get?

Charles (*grittily changing the subject*) Where—is my blue shirt?

Norma In the laundry basket—which reminds me . . . (*She gets up to look out of the window*) I wonder if I should ask him.

Charles Ask who?

Norma The chap across at number nine—the one whose wife seems to have disappeared.

Charles What about him?

Norma I mean that wonderful woman who was doing his step. Do you know, I saw her hanging out about three hundred yards of washing this morning? I wonder where he got her? I mean, if I knew, it might save me putting an advertisement in the paper.

David hurries into the living-room. He is carrying a yellow plastic basket, full of washing and with pegs clipped along the top. He looks around, checking, sees the vacuum cleaner and grabs it and hurriedly exits as:

Keith starts getting out of bed

Susan Where are you going now?
Keith (*indicating his mug*) More tea. How about you?
Susan (*sharply*) No. (*But she manages a little smile*) No thanks.

Keith exits from the bedroom to the landing, taking his mug with him

Susan sits a moment, then retrieves her cigarettes and lights one as:

Norma returns to the table to fuss with her new tree. Charles sits, crossing his legs to untie the plunger

Charles You're just not taking this business seriously, are you?
Norma It's supposed to be fun.
Charles Fun? A bloody fancy dress party full of people I've never met and you call that fun?
Norma They're very nice I'm sure they are.
Charles *You* only know Peter and he's a pain in the neck.
Norma I know the hostess.
Charles And who do I know?
Norma Don't be so stuffy. He'll be picking us up at eight by the way.
Charles Will he.
Norma I thought if we went in his car you could relax and have a few drinks.

There's nothing he can moan about there, so:

Charles What's the stupid idea anyway—fancy dress.
Norma It's to get things going.
Charles What's wrong with a large Scotch?
Norma It's to give people who don't know each other something to talk about. Honestly Charles, you're worse than some of your patients— stop complaining and simply look on it as a fun idea. Like you did your sister's wedding.
Charles I knew her.
Norma Only just.

He scowls at her

Well you're not the closest family in the world, are you darling?
Charles People of our age . . .
Norma People of your age—yes?
Charles People of my age do not wear fancy dress.
Norma Of course they do. (*She carefully takes up her tree*)
Charles Name three.
Norma I don't know their names but they'll be there tonight, I promise you.

She delicately relieves him of the scarf and exits into the garage with her handbag and her precious tree

Charles sits moodily for a moment, then exits into the garage, taking the sink plunger with him, as:

Keith enters the bedroom with the mug and gets back into bed

Keith She's back.
Susan Who is? (*She guiltily stubs out her cigarette*)
Keith That nice-looking one at number nine. Came in a taxi. *He* was waiting outside for her. Looked a right bag of nerves.
Susan Maybe she left him and thought better of it. (*Flatly*) We could be on the verge of our very first scandal.
Keith Mind you, when he saw me looking, he actually gave me a wave. Well a sort of a wave.
Susan Perhaps he would have liked a meal or something while she was away—we should have asked him over.
Keith Flipping 'eck, Sue, we don't even know the man.
Susan Well he did wave.
Keith You're right. He did wave. Next thing you know we'll be talking.

And they remain, each with their own thoughts as:

Hilary enters the living-room. She's attractive, looks and feels incredibly well. She takes off her light summer coat, looking around the room, pleased to be home. As she throws the coat over the sofa, she sees the plant. She smiles fondly, and takes up the plant to smell it

David enters with her weekend suitcase

Hilary (*turning and indicating the plant*) It's lovely. Thank you.

He stops then puts down the suitcase and with an expansive gesture

David Welcome home.
Hilary And thank you for letting me indulge myself.

They kiss

David It was worth it: you look terrific.

She sits on the sofa, returning the plant to the table as he moves round to casually glance from the "window"

Hilary (*patting her stomach*) Five and a half pounds.
David Well done.
Hilary One of the women lost ten. The cow.
David You do, you look terrific.

He sits next to her. She puts an arm around his waist, snuggling against him

Hilary I feel terrific, I really do.
David Yes, you really do.

They again kiss, briefly this time. She remains with her head on his shoulder

Hilary (*smiling at the sudden thought of*) What did you tell your mother?
David Sorry?
Hilary I hope you didn't tell her I was at a health farm.
David (*brightly*) Course not. (*His face changes*) I told her you were in hospital.
Hilary I was in hospital three months ago.

David I said you were having a check-up. Hil——
Hilary How strange—you've broken my dream.
David What dream?
Hilary I had this very strange dream. I suppose I must have been hallucinating on the lemon juice. I was in hospital . . . lying on the operating table . . . and I looked up and there was this surgeon with a huge knife . . . only it wasn't a surgeon, it was you, smiling, god-like . . . and I thought how wonderful, not only does he pay the rates he's going to save my life . . . which you were just about to do when the door burst open and in came your mother. She grabbed the knife and said, "That's all right, son, I'll carve" . . . and she did . . . and the pair of you sat down and . . .
David Oi—come on, Ada. (*He kisses her brow lightly and gets up to again look casually out of the "window"*)
Hilary Yes, you're quite right, I don't want to talk about her, we'll only end up arguing.
David She's not that bad.
Hilary She's awful. Anyway, I don't care what she thinks. I was rundown, I needed a rest and thanks to you I got one . . . What are you looking for?
David What? Oh . . . it's that young couple with the twins.
Hilary What about them?
David They've still got their curtains drawn.
Hilary How terrible.
David Well it's Saturday—last two Saturdays he's been up at the crack of dawn mucking about with that old motor bike of his.
Hilary You can't *see* their windows from here—what are you on about?
David (*moving from the "window"*) Tell you what, Hil: we ought to introduce ourselves then maybe I could borrow his ladder.
Hilary What d'you want a ladder for?
David What I mean is, if I ever needed one. (*Brightly*) Right then, what d'you fancy—I mean, anything you'd especially like to do?
Hilary (*standing*) Well, it's a nice day—why don't we make a start on the garden?
David You hate gardening.
Hilary I need to keep moving—it takes my mind off food. (*She takes up the plant and her coat*) Which reminds me: I'm buying a bike. (*She moves towards the door*)
David God, all that energy.
Hilary (*at the door*) Can we go out tonight?
David Er . . . why not?
Hilary You can chat me up over a green salad.

She pouts a provocative kiss and exits

David glances out of the "window", sighs, then exits as:

In the bedroom:

Susan Christ.

Keith (*lowering his newspaper*) What's happened?
Susan I forgot to pack their macs.
Keith Their what?
Susan In case it rains. (*With a change of tone*) Sorry. (*Changing the subject*)
Can we go to the pictures first, then have a meal?
Keith Certainly.
Susan It doesn't affect anything, does it?
Keith Well I'll miss *Match of the Day* but that won't kill me, will it?
Course it doesn't affect anything, you daft lump.
Susan (*her head on his shoulder*) We haven't been to the pictures for ages.
Keith Ask me what's on.
Susan What's on?
Keith Aha!

*He holds up the newspaper with an exaggerated flourish so that they are
both out of sight behind it*

The Palace Cinema. Studio One . . . *Sexy Schoolteacher* and *Return of
the Flasher* . . . Studio Two . . . *Confessions of a Naughty Nun* and *Altar
of Desire* . . . Studio Three . . . *Savage Connections* and *I Was a Teenage
Sex Maniac in a Swedish Massage Parlour*.
Susan What's on at the Odeon?

The paper shakes violently

Keith *Snow White and the Seven Dwarfs*. (*He lowers the paper*) So then,
what d'you fancy?
Susan Well I quite fancy the Teenage Sex Maniac in the Swedish Massage
Parlour.
Keith (*with pleasure*) You don't.
Susan Yes I do.
Keith (*derisively*) Swedish Massage Parlour.
Susan P'raps it'll give us a few ideas.
Keith You dirty devil.
Susan We could certainly do with them just lately, couldn't we? Or at
least *I* could.

*She has tried to make it sound light, but it's too near the truth. He therefore
tries to make it sound even lighter*

Keith If you're not careful I shall go out and buy a couple of mucky books.
Susan Go on then—dare you.
Keith I will.
Susan Go on then—I dare you.
Keith Here—what goes on when I'm out working all day?
Susan You'd be surprised.
Keith I knew we should never have moved on to one of these estates.
Susan That's a laugh, no-one ever talks to you.
Keith They wave, don't they, what more do you want? Give it a chance,
love, we've only been in a month.

Susan You don't think we made a mistake do you Keith, buying this house?
Keith Hey.

Another delicate subject. A moment. But then she snuggles up against him

Susan We· ought to make a start on the garden this weekend. We've had some snotty looks from the neighbours.
Keith You can't call them neighbours just because they live next door. Neighbours is something quite different.
Susan I wonder what they're thinking.
Keith Who?
Susan The neighbours. Two o'clock and the curtains still drawn.
Keith Dunno. Don't care really.
Susan They all look so—organized.

David quickly enters the kitchen from the hall with the plant. He looks around, looks at the plant, not knowing what to do with it

Hilary (*calling; off*) Where are you?
David Er . . . (*Calling back*) Looking for the spade.

He looks at the plant, then opens one of the top cupboards, shoves the plant inside and exits into the garage

Susan Probably think we're a couple of sex-maniacs. If only they knew.
Keith *Susie.*

She buries her head into his shoulder, squeezing her eyes shut

Susan This is really nice, isn't it? Really nice.

A moment. Then he puts an arm around her, kisses her brow. She snuggles even closer and he gives her another kiss

Keith Tell you what: this weekend we'll make a positive effort to put ourselves about a bit, see if we can meet someone for you.
Susan Not this weekend. This weekend I want it to be just you and me. Just . . . doing nothing. Maybe if I could just . . . you know . . . maybe it'd be all right again.
Keith Course it will, you daft ha'p'orth. (*He kisses her brow briefly*) I love you. Course it'll be all right.

She smiles, still with her eyes closed, still arms about him like a child. A moment

Gotta get the car taxed next week.
Susan (*eyes still closed*) More money.
Keith I won't do it for the whole year. Just the six months. I'll have the bike back on the road by then.

Her eyes open momentarily, then close again. He smiles to himself, warming to his pride and joy

I mean . . . a car's all right . . . but nothing like a good bike. We had some wonderful holidays on that bike, didn't we?

Susan (*flatly*). Wonderful.

Keith Yeah . . . it'll be just like the old days. Off to Scotland or somewhere . . . you on the back . . .

Susan You're forgetting the twins.

Keith No I'm not. Which is why I'm re-building the sidecar.

Susan (*eyes opening, suddenly aware*) You don't mean today, Keith, you're
not going to start doing it *today*?

Keith Course not love. I'm just saying.

*A moment. Then, satisfied, she closes her eyes again, snuggling close to him.
He sits looking straight ahead as:*

> *Hilary enters the kitchen from the hall. She has changed into more casual
> clothing. She stands, looking round the kitchen. There is an air of amused
> satisfaction about her. She sniffs the sink, flips at the serviette under the
> toaster, and nods to herself, her satisfaction seemingly increased. She
> shakes the kettle, checking that it contains water and is about to open the
> cupboard in which David put the plant when:*

> *David enters the kitchen from the garage*

David I thought we had *two* spades . . . What are you doing?

*She turns, the cupboard open now so that the plant can be seen in solitary
splendour*

Hilary Looking for the cups.

David (*moving quickly to close the cupboard door*) Whaffor?

Hilary Because I fancy a cup of tea before we start—how about you?

David (*ushering her away*) I'll do it—you sit down.

*She sits at the table, her back to him, but turns to watch as he opens another
cupboard, reaching in his hand confidently, but checking on finding the cupboard full of tins. He opens the next cupboard to find it full of glasses. He
peers round the corner of the cupboard, as though the cups might be lurking
somewhere in there, but realizes that Hilary is watching him, amused*

I—changed things round. (*He indicates expansively*) Did a sort of—time
and motion.

Hilary (*mock-impressed*) I can see.

*She deliberately turns away from him. He opens another cupboard in desper-
ate pursuit of the cups as:*

> *In the bedroom, Keith slips quietly out of bed, leaving the now-sleeping
> Susan. He takes up the tray and exits quietly from the bedroom, closing
> the door*

I bet you didn't remember to cancel the milk.

David Oh yes I did—and I remembered to start it again. Cups cups cups . . .

Hilary David.

David Yes love.

Hilary There's a serviette under the toaster, blue water down the lavatory,

half a gallon of Jeyes Fluid down the sink and the airing cupboard's
been tampered with—your mother's been, hasn't she?
David (*very firmly*) As a matter of fact, yes she has.
Hilary Fine. That's all you had to say.

*She smiles, gets up and moves to the sink to empty the teapot. David is
completely taken aback*

David *I* thought—while you were away—well you know how she's been
nagging me about seeing the new house . . .
Hilary Good idea. She gets to see the house and I don't get to see *her.*
(*Looking through the window*) Oh God, she's planting a tree.
David (*misconstruing*) Who is?
Hilary The one with the plastic pond.
David (*relieved*) Oh, the doctor's wife. Hil——
Hilary Oh God, she looks so bloody efficient. I bet she makes her own
yoghurt. (*She looks at him*) You're not sorry we moved, are you?
David It'll be fine.

She looks at him, then kisses him lightly

Hilary You should have the children over.
David Next weekend I thought. (*With a slight edge*) It's my weekend,
anyway.
Hilary It'll get better when they're older. They can make up their own
minds. (*She again kisses him lightly*) I think there *is* only one spade,
come to think of it . . .

She exits into the garage

David The thing is . . . when I say "been" . . .

A moment

Hilary slowly reappears

(*Polishing his glasses*) I mean . . . when I say she's been . . .
Hilary You mean she's still here. (*Her attitude is pure ice now*)
David I thought you were coming back tomorrow.
Hilary Where is she?
David (*an attempt at firmness*) She's doing the shopping.
Hilary *I* see.
David I wanted her out of the way so that we could . . . discuss the
situation.

The front doorbell rings

Oh gawd.
Hilary (*brightly*) That'll be *her*, will it?
David I dunno . . . probably.
Hilary Right. (*She moves to the hall door*) *You* go and let your mother in,
I'm going to bed.
David Waddaya mean—bed?
Hilary (*holding her smile*) I feel faint.

David But you've just spent a week in a health farm . . .

The doorbell rings again

Shut up!

Hilary No, no—I've just spent a week in hospital. And I feel faint. (*And, still holding the smile, she aims a solitary but violent kick at the nearest cabinet*)

David But you can't go to bed—now *now*.

Hilary As long as *she*'s here I can—believe me.

She smiles and exits

David (*shouting after her*) Why won't you ever *listen*!

Mrs Hinson appears outside the kitchen window, tapping at it

David turns, to see her gesticulating through the window. He gives a hopeless gesture of defeat and moves to open the garage door

Mrs Hinson Why don't you people ever answer the door?

David *Because.*

Mrs Hinson (*confidentially*) Everything all right, is it son?

David Couldn't . . . be . . . better.

Mrs Hinson What did I say? (*She pecks his cheek*) Come and give me a hand with the shopping.

David Where is it?

Mrs Hinson I left it round the front. My arms are like lead . . .

David All we wanted was a *loaf.*

Mrs Hinson Don't matter about that . . . I got you a few extras . . .

They exit into the garage, David closing the door as:

Norma enters the living-room. She is carrying a notepad and pencil. Her hair, now in rollers, is covered by a hair-drying plastic hood. She sits on the sofa and begins to jot notes

After a moment, Charles enters the living-room. He is wearing a red vest over a black nylon roll-neck sweater, old white rugby shorts over black tights, a curtain (still with the wooden rings in) as a cape, wellington boots, gardening gloves, and a mask made out of a Sainsbury's bag. It's the third outfit he's tried on and he is just about maintaining his civility. He moves to stand by the sofa and strikes a half-hearted pose

Norma doesn't look up, so Charles nudges her with a boot. She looks up. He again strikes his pose. She remains looking at him for a moment, her face expressionless

Norma How does this sound? (*She reads her notes*) "Domestic Help required, four hours per week, excellent wages."

Charles What about *this*?

Again he poses. A moment

Norma Very good. What are you supposed to be this time?

Charles (*enunciating irritably*) Batman.

Norma Well that's all right then, isn't it? (*She regards her notes*) Perhaps I should say it's a new house.
Charles (*taking off his mask*) Well then. That's me fixed.
Norma (*looking up, frowning*) Are those my ballet tights?
Charles Now look here: are we absolutely agreed that I should go as Batman.
Norma Absolutely.
Charles Because I'm not trying on anything else, Norma, this is my third outfit and I'm not going through it all again.
Norma No darling, you look lovely.
Charles Batman it is then.
Norma Lovely. (*She returns to her notes*)
Charles (*hovering*) I'm not asking you to go as Robin.
Norma Of course you're not, you're not the type.

He looks down at himself, gives a few desultory flaps of the cape

Charles (*gloomily*) I suppose it'll be quite fun, really.
Norma Of course it will.
Charles Bit of a laugh and everything.
Norma Do you good.
Charles (*regarding the gardening gloves*) I can probably improve on the gloves.
Norma Yes, I seem to remember Batman climbing up walls, I can't remember him doing a great deal of gardening.
Charles So the same thing would probably apply to the wellies. (*He regards them*)
Norma I would have thought so.
Charles What I really need . . . is a pair of riding boots.
Norma Ask that young chap across at number eleven.
Charles Does he ride?
Norma He's got a motor bike, so he must have a pair of boots.
Charles I'm supposed to be The Caped Crusader. I mean, dammit all, put a pair of those things on and you automatically start kicking people to death.
Norma Don't be so intolerant.
Charles (*peering through the "curtains"*) Depends what you expect me to tolerate.
Norma Not much.
Charles Mind you. If he's got a motor bike, he's probably got a decent pair of gloves. Gauntlets.
Norma What a good idea. Then you could throw one down and pick a fight with someone.
Charles I could what?
Norma Well you know how aggressive you get when there are more than three people in the room.
Charles You don't throw down the gauntlet to pick a fight with someone, you throw it down as a challenge.
Norma Yes of course you do, silly me.

Charles (*peering through the "curtains"*) I wonder if I should?

Norma Go on—pop across and ask him.

Charles He's got a car.

Norma And a motor bike.

Charles *I've* never seen a motor bike over there.

Norma It looks very old: rather like that disgusting thing you wanted me to straddle before my father intervened.

Charles That disgusting thing as you call it was a Brough Superior.

Norma Was it really.

Charles And for your information, Lawrence of Arabia *died* on a Brough Superior.

Norma Then he should have stuck to camels.

During the next few speeches, as Norma and Charles continue talking, Keith—now dressed—enters the kitchen from the garage. His sleeves are rolled up, his hands are oily, and he is examining a carburettor. He takes up a clean tea-towel and wipes the carburettor with it as, totally pre-occupied and happy, he exits into the garage

Charles (*peering through the "curtains" again*) I wonder why I've never seen it?

Norma He keeps it in the garage: I think he's doing it up or something.

Charles Well then: you can't be sure he rides it.

Norma I saw him. One afternoon. He couldn't get it started so he shouted at his wife.

In the bedroom, Susan sits up in bed with the sudden realization that Keith has gone

Susan Keith?

She gets out of bed and moves to peer down from the "window", so that she is looking down and Charles is looking up

Charles The curtains are still drawn.

Norma (*firmly*) Go across and ask him.

Charles hesitates, but moves away from the "window"

At the same time, Susan takes a dressing-gown from the wardrobe and exits from the bedroom

Charles No, I don't think so. Anyway, we've never spoken to them.

Norma Then you'll break the ice.

Charles I don't like speaking to people. That's the trouble with these bloody estates, people expect you to speak to them. Next thing you know, some twerp will form a residents' association and it'll be all whist drives and gardening competitions.

Norma It's not that kind of estate and anyway they're not called estates any more.

Charles Well what are they called? (*He practices a few Batman swoops behind the sofa*)

Norma I don't know, but they're not called estates. Not an estate like this one isn't. This is called a twelve-unit development—or something like that, I can't quite remember but anyway Mr Thingy the estate agent told me—well *you* should know.

Charles *I* call it an estate.

Norma Estate is a very common word.

Charles Are you implying that I'm common?

Norma I'm saying you *were* common.

Charles I was.

Norma You were.

Charles And when did I stop being common?

Norma The day you married *me*, darling.

She smiles and takes off the cap, revealing the rollers. She passes the cap to Charles and takes out the rollers, mechanically handing each one to Charles who mechanically takes it and drops it into the cap

Charles Have you any idea what *you're* going as?

Norma Not yet.

Charles (*patiently*) Norma—it is tonight.

Norma I'll think of something.

Charles Well shouldn't we sort of start—narrowing it down?

Norma How d'you mean?

Charles Well if I'm going as Batman, shouldn't you complement me or something?

Norma I've already said—you look lovely.

Charles Not compliment—complement.

Norma Give me a for example.

Charles Well . . . for example . . . you could go as Wonder Woman.

Norma Go as I am, you mean.

Charles I'm trying to be helpful.

Norma What a very tidy mind you must have, Charles—seeing us as a pair. Or are you just an old romantic—letting everyone know that I'm your woman and hands off?

Charles I was trying—to be helpful.

Norma Yes, I'm afraid you were.

Charles digs into the pocket of his shorts to pull out his pipe

Charles Well. I've done my bit.

Norma Don't—sulk.

Charles What we should have done is hired something. That's what every-one else will have done. None of your bits of tat. It'll be all crinolines and clowns and Twenty-second Hussars, you see if I'm not right.

Norma I shouldn't think so for one minute.

Charles You'll see. (*He raps his pipe on his wellington*)

Norma Besides, where's the sense of achievement in hiring something? Think of the great warm feeling you got when you finally settled on Batman. Apart from anything else, it lets everyone know you've bothered. Anyone can *hire*.

Charles I'll tell you something else: suppose we're the only ones? You

might have made a mistake, it might not be fancy dress at all—oh my
God what a thought—give her a ring this friend of yours and find out.
Norma Don't be silly darling, it's on the invitation.
Charles My first weekend off in two months and look at me. (*But an even
worse thought*) What happens if I'm not the only Batman?
Norma What d'you mean, what happens?
Charles Suppose there are two of us? Batmen. Mans. Right bloody fool
I'm going to look. There could even be six of us. Ten.
Norma Then you'll just have to hang on the ceiling out of everyone's way,
won't you? (*She takes up the cap and makes to go out, but, pleasantly*)
And you can take that lot off: you look bloody ridiculous.

Norma exits from the living-room as;

*Hilary, in a night-dress, enters the bedroom from the bathroom, turns off
the bedside light and gets into bed, so that the bedroom is in darkness as:*

*Susan enters the kitchen from the hall. She is wearing the dressing-gown.
She reaches into a cupboard, takes out a large biscuit tin and moves to
open the garage door. We hear the sound of Keith banging away, whistling
cheerfully. Satisfied, she closes the door and sits at the table. She takes out
a biscuit and is chewing on it mechanically, cradling the tin which is her
comforter as:*

Keith enters from the garage, carrying the stained tea-towel, still whistling

Keith Hello love, I was just going to bring you another cup of tea.

*He drops the towel on to the table, takes a tin of Swarfega from beneath the
sink, rubs some into his hands and washes it off as Susan takes up the filthy
tea-towel by its corner, then lets it drop back on to the table*

Anyway. I found out why she wouldn't start.
Susan Oh?
Keith Dirt in the float chamber, simple as that.
Susan You had dirt in your float chamber once before, I seem to re-
member.
Keith (*incredulously*) Did I?
Susan That time on the Isle of Man. It was raining.
Keith Oh yeah: four hours I spent under that bike.

Charles exits from the living-room

Susan Still. You did meet that man who'd just come second in the big
race. You had your photograph taken with him. He let you sit on his
bike.
Keith (*his face brightening*) Oh yeah: that four-cylinder two-stroke
Yamaha Seven-fifty. Where *are* my photographs?

*He moves to take up the tea-towel. She pointedly holds it up with two fingers.
He takes the tea-towel—her point missed—and dries his hands*

Susan You said you wanted them in safekeeping so I asked the man to
put them straight up in the loft.

Keith What, my medals and everything?
Susan It's all right, they're still in the box.
Keith Only sooner or later I shall want to make up my display . . . nice
bit of wall somewhere . . . (*he mimes*) . . . photographs . . . my medals
. . . that autographed Barry Sheene poster . . . waddaya think?
Susan I think I shall have a bath. (*She makes to go out*)
Keith Oh come on love, I did try to stay in bed but you know me, it's a
physical impossibility.
Susan Then why did you *say*?
Keith I know, I know.
Susan You get rid of the kids and then you spend all your time mucking
about with that stupid rotten motor bike.
Keith I didn't get rid of them—but you're quite right, I shouldn't be
doing the bike, it's just that when I start something . . .
Susan Then you shouldn't have started something, should you? *Should
you*?

She's genuinely upset and he knows it

Keith No, I shouldn't.
Susan If you want to start something, if you've got to start something,
you should start something on the house . . .
Keith I *do*.
Susan No. You talk about doing it—like you talk about . . . everything
else—but you never actually *do* anything.
Keith I put that shelf up.
Susan One shelf.
Keith It's a start.
Susan It fell down and it stays down.
Keith I keep telling you—the plaster's still alive.
Susan Well bully for the plaster!

A moment

Keith Look, you're absolutely right and I'm very sorry.
Susan (*brusquely*) So am I.

A moment

Oh listen to me, I'm nagging you again.
Keith No.
Susan I am, I'm nagging you.
Keith No you're not.
Susan I *am*, I *know* I am.
Keith Give us a kiss and shut up.

*They kiss and remain with their arms about each other, then she smiles up at
him, gives him another brief kiss and makes to go out as:*

*Charles enters the living-room, now stripped to the waist and wearing the
shorts, tights and wellingtons. He takes up the bag/mask and the gloves,
makes to go out, but then looks at the gloves and moves to peer from the*

"window", *considering whether or not to go across and ask Keith about gauntlets*

Susan You know that couple across the road.

Keith Which couple?

Susan I think someone said he was a doctor.

Keith Oh him, yeah, what about him?

Susan He keeps looking over here.

Keith He what?

Susan I saw him: he was peering through their sitting-room window.

Keith Doctors don't peer, do they, only down your ears.

Susan He was though. I had another look a bit later and he was doing it again.

Keith P'raps he's a pervert: Peeping Tom's delight, an estate like this. (*He grins but nevertheless has a look through the kitchen window*)

Charles exits from the living-room

Susan You can't see him from there, silly.

Keith I can see his pond though. And his bloody great car blocking up the road. Look at it, bloody great Lancia. *And* a Renault Five for Madam. Do all right, don't they, these doctors.

Susan I expect he's a specialist or something.

Keith No, they're all the same nowadays, these doctors. And dentists, they're even worse. Who's ever heard of a starving dentist?

Susan I'm sure they're very nice.

Keith I'm sure they are. (*He kisses her brow*) Not as nice as you though.

Susan I think she works.

Keith Well her arms and legs move, I dunno about the rest of her.

Susan In the town hall I think. The one next door works, I know. She's got a briefcase. (*With a touch of envy*) P'raps she wasn't on holiday, p'raps she was at a conference. (*With a change of tone*) If we're going to eat later I think we should book a table.

Keith I'll pop down the road and give 'em a ring.

Susan You're quite sure we can afford it.

Keith You've got to stop thinking we're skint.

Susan Well we are, aren't we?

Keith Yes, but you've got to stop thinking it. You've got to think positive.

Susan Right. First thing tomorrow morning I'm starting my diet. (*She returns the biscuit tin to its place*)

Keith Absolutely.

Susan I mean it. (*She pulls at her dressing-gown*) Look at me. I'm so ugly.

Keith You might not have a briefcase but one thing you do have is a beautiful body—go and get in the bath—and leave the door open.

Susan You won't forget to give them a ring, will you?

Keith This very minute. (*He takes a coin from his pocket and holds it up to prove his intention*)

Susan smiles and exits to the hall

Keith whistles his way to the garage door but stops to call back

Keith Sue?

Susan (*calling; off*) Yes?

Keith Whereabouts in the loft?

Susan (*calling; off*) Sorry?

Keith Doesn't matter . . . doesn't matter . . .

He frowns, pocketing the coin, and exits into the garage

The bedroom is still in darkness, but then light spills in from the landing as David puts his head round the door and enters the bedroom quietly. He moves round to the bed, trying to be very quiet

Hilary Oh stop creeping about and put the light on, you stupid little person.

He goes back and turns on the main light. Hilary is lying flat on her back, staring rigidly at the ceiling. Only her head is visible, on one pillow, the others having been tossed to one side

Hilary How long has she been staying here?

David Yesterday.

Hilary Liar.

David Tuesday.

Hilary How did she know?

David Know what?

Hilary That *I*'d left you all on your own, you sly little twerp.

David I phoned her—Monday like I always phone her on a Monday— and, obviously I told her you were—in hospital.

Hilary And, obviously, she was on the first train.

David Now be fair, Hil, we see her twice a year. At the most.

Hilary And both times she stays four months. At the least.

David That isn't true. It only feels like four months.

Hilary It feels like ten months and there's no "only" about it. *That*'s why you wanted me to go away, so *she* could come.

David *I* wanted you . . .?

Hilary When I think . . . all the time I was lying there, starving myself senseless for *your* benefit, she was here, waltzing around in her stupid pinnie, stuffing you full of tinned fruit and her rotten rice pudding—does she know you're forty years old?

David She's my mother. I'm her only son for Chrissake. What am I supposed to do, ignore her? Have her put down like your stupid bloody dachshund?

Hilary What you're supposed to do is get your priorities right. You live with *me*.

David (*angrily*) I'll take her home now—all right? I'll take her home *now*. (*He makes for the door*)

Hilary Why don't you take her to the Blessed Rosemary?

David (*wearily*) Don't bring her into it, please.

Hilary Oh she of little faith and a great deal of maintenance—well she
can have you—they both can—with my best wishes—oh . . . go away.
*(Genuinely upset, she turns on her side, dragging the duvet up over her
head)*
David *(sitting on the bed)* I had it all worked out. I was going to take her
home tomorrow morning. But when you phoned and said you were
coming home today . . . well . . . it all got screwed up.

A moment. Then Hilary pushes the duvet back

Hilary Every time we see her we end up . . .
David *(kissing her gently)* I know, I know . . .
Hilary *(taking his hand)* It's not *her* that upsets me so much . . . it's what
she does to *you*.
David Hey . . . *(he kisses her again)* . . . I'll take her home—and until I do
—no more interference, promise.

They are about to kiss when:

*Mrs Hinson enters the bedroom busily. She is wearing her pinnie and
carries her handbag, a hot-water bottle and a duster*

Mrs Hinson You forgot the hot-water bottle, you naughty boy.

*On hearing the dreaded voice, Hilary breaks away from David and struggles
into an upright position, beaming hugely*

Hilary Hello *Mum*—how are you? Nice to see you.
Mrs Hinson Nice to see *you*, dear.

They are so pleasant to each other, it hurts

David Mum . . . she doesn't *want* a hot water bottle.
Mrs Hinson *(waving him away)* Oh don' matter about that, the girl's sick,
she needs looking after—oh look at those pillows—why didn't you do
the 'pillows for her, David? *(She swings into action, rather roughly
pushing Hilary forward to arrange the pillows in a pile at her back)* I've
just been tidying up.
Hilary How clever of you to bring your pinnie.
Mrs Hinson How's that?
Hilary Thanks Mum, that's lovely.

*Behind Mrs Hinson's back, Hilary gives a huge V-sign at David. Mrs
Hinson levers Hilary back against the wall of pillows*

Mrs Hinson David says you're not eating.
David She doesn't *want* to eat.
Mrs Hinson *(to Hilary, ignoring him)* How about a nice cup of milky
coffee?
Hilary Mmm . . . *lovely*.
Mrs Hinson *(to David)* Go on then, off you go.
David *(through gritted teeth)* Mum . . . I told you . . . to stay . . . away.
Mrs Hinson We want a little chat—isn't that right, Hilary?

Hilary *Mmmm—(she beams at David)*—off you go, you naughty boy.

David hesitates a moment, teeth bared, but throws up his arms and exits

Mrs Hinson moves to the door to call after him

Mrs Hinson And bring her up one of those nice apples I bought! (*To Hilary*) Thirty-eight p a pound—that's nearly eight shillings in real money—but what does that matter when it's for someone you love? (*She closes the door and speaks in a manner that is more mouthing than actually saying the words, as though not wanting to be overheard. This is always her manner when talking "delicate"*) I thought he was looking very tired.

Hilary Did you?

Mrs Hinson You know—mentally. I think he could do with a good holiday myself. It must be a terrible strain, being executive. Still. You're a great help to him, I know you are. When you're fit.

Hilary (*smiling*) Been looking after him for me, have you Mum?

Mrs Hinson I thought you might be upset, me staying here.

Hilary Upset? *Heavens!*

They "smile" at each other as:

David enters the kitchen from the hall. He glares around impotently, then remembers the plant and furtively takes it out of the cupboard as:

Mrs Hinson I would have visited you, but David intimated that he'd rather see you all to himself.

Hilary Yes, he can be very forceful.

David (*shouting at the ceiling*) If that's what you want, get on with it, the pair of you!

But he looks down at the plant, wondering what to do with it, then on impulse shoves it into the cupboard under the sink, and exits into the hall as:

Mrs Hinson (*intimate again*) He never told me what it was, you know: didn't want to worry me, I expect. Something internal, was it dear?

Hilary Vaguely.

Mrs Hinson You was internal before, I seem to remember.

Hilary Yes, I think I was.

Mrs Hinson It's usually internal with a woman. Mine was internal, you know.

Hilary Well I never knew that.

Mrs Hinson That was before all these drugs of course. (*She sucks in air dramatically, re-living the moment*) I could have gone either way. The entire profession was dumbfounded apparently.

Hilary Oh dear.

Again they "smile" at each other

Mrs Hinson I was noticing how brown you look.

Hilary (*like Red Riding Hood*) What big *eyes* you've got.

Mrs Hinson Put you near a window, did they dear—or was it the ultra-violet?

Hilary I think everything looks better with a tan—don't you? Even sliced bread.

Mrs Hinson I know this much—you've lost weight.

Hilary Nearly six pounds.

Mrs Hinson (*sucking in air*) You'll need building up then—can't have *both* of you walking about looking half-starved.

Hilary Thanks for doing the airing cupboard by the way, that was really useful.

Mrs Hinson That's all right dear, I did your drawers as well.

Hilary How *do* you manage and you with that terrible migraine?

Mrs Hinson (*intimate again*) I couldn't help noticing the state of his underwear—well, they're falling to pieces—so I popped down to Marks and got him some new ones. They do a lovely selection nowadays. You can use the old ones for dusters. You seem quite short of dusters, don't you dear?

Hilary But not now though, eh Mum? (*She smiles*)

Mrs Hinson gets up and flits around the bedhead with her duster

Mrs Hinson Yes, well, you keep yourself wrapped up, there's a lot of it about. (*She makes to go, but*) I'm making you a lovely steak and kidney pudding—that'll build you up a bit . . . oh no, you don't like my puddings, do you?

Hilary Sorry.

Mrs Hinson Not your fault, dear, I expect my David will manage to force it down, he loves my puddings. (*She makes to go out again*) Yes, he's a good boy, my David, for all his funny ways. That last wife of his, that Rosemary . . . she was a strange one, she was, couldn't cook for toffees. Mind you, she did his shirts beautiful. Oh yes, I've got those snaps I was telling you about . . . that house we all took in Bournemouth that summer . . . that was a lovely holiday that was, oh yes, the two children were so happy—well they love being with their father—that was in the August, just prior to him meeting you in the September and deserting them in the October . . . now where are they . . .? (*She advances on Hilary, searching her handbag for the photographs*)

Hilary Excuse me . . . I suddenly feel quite sick.

She gets out of bed and exits into the bathroom, pointedly slamming the door behind her

Unperturbed, Mrs Hinson re-pockets her little album of photographs

Mrs Hinson Yes that's all right dear—make yourself comfortable. I'll just pop down and see how my David's making out in the kitchen. You know what they're like—helpless and hopeless. (*But, to herself*) He shouldn't have to *be* in the kitchen, man in his position.

Mrs Hinson exits from the bedroom, as:

Charles enters the living-room. He wears a blond wig, a long evening dress in electric blue with a boa and matching shoulder-strap evening bag, and is carrying a long cigarette holder. He is feeling quite pleased with himself. He turns and moves to the cabinet to take out a bottle of sherry. As he does we see that the evening dress is straining across his broad back and is fastened by a criss-cross of white football laces

Norma enters. She is dressed as a schoolgirl. A straw hat, slightly too big for her—her son's old school blazer, shirt and tie—a short black skirt, stockings and high-heel shoes. She feels ridiculous

Norma (*irritably*) Well?

Charles turns to regard her as she strikes a half-hearted pose, glowering at him

Charles What are you supposed to be?
Norma Oh don't be so smug, it's obvious what I'm supposed to be, isn't it—a Ronald Thingy schoolgirl—what are *you* supposed to be?

He puts one foot up on the chair, revealing brown brogues and nasty short socks and strikes a pose with the cigarette holder

Charles Marlene Dietrich.
Norma (*flatly*) Marlene Dietrich.
Charles Good eh?
Norma *Falling In Love Again*. With a moustache.
Charles But that's the whole point, don't you see?
Norma No I don't bloody see.
Charles Simple . . . effective . . . and satirical. Good eh?
Norma Am I going like this or aren't I? (*She sits, glowering, cross-legged, on the sofa*)
Charles As a schoolgirl.
Norma I've already said. God, you can be so irritating.

He regards her for a moment

Charles No I don't think so, Norma, thank you.
Norma What d'you mean, you don't think so?
Charles I mean I'm not walking to the car with you dressed like that . . . be it a Ronald Thingy schoolgirl or any other kind of schoolgirl.
Norma But it's all right for you to walk to the car looking like a pair of my best curtains.
Charles (*sitting next to her*) I'm not thinking of me, Norma, I'm thinking of you.
Norma (*with a rising edge*) I see. You think I'm getting fat.
Charles I have never said . . .
Norma That's why you don't want me to go as a schoolgirl, you're ashamed of my thighs.
Charles It's you who keeps going on about your thighs. I happen to rather like them that size.
Norma *What* size?
Charles I *like* them.

Norma All right. I'll go as something else. How does a WVS lady suit you? Or a nun. Do nuns show their thighs? I can't remember, it's so long since we went to church.

Charles Now just a minute . . . just a minute . . . I've had an idea. I'll go as you and you go as me.

Norma I'm not going.

Charles Course you are. Have a sherry. (*He goes to the drinks cabinet. He takes up the sherry bottle, but does not quite get round to pouring her a drink*)

Norma I am not going.

Charles Why not?

Norma Because we should have hired, that's why not.

Charles Oh come on Norma, it'll be fun.

Norma It's all right for you, you look ridiculous whatever you wear.

Charles (*moving back to her with the bottle*) Tell you what: *you* go as Batman and . . .

Norma The only reason I said I'd go to this rotten party is because *you* wanted to meet some of my new friends. Because *you* haven't got any new friends. You haven't got any *old* ones. The only friends we've got— the only friends we've ever had—are my friends. You're so bloody *miserable*.

Charles That is not often true.

Norma You couldn't even be pleasant to your own son which is why as soon as he got his driving licence he was off and I hope it's made you very happy because it hasn't *me*.

Charles Our son left home because he was twenty-two years old and pre- ferred living in a squat with a cross-bred collie and a drum-kit.

Norma I don't wish to talk about it.

Charles (*sighing*) I knew we'd end up arguing. My first weekend off in two months. I knew we should have gone away somewhere.

Norma You always get a cold when we go away—it's the shock of actually spending money.

Charles Oh I see . . . that's the latest is it, I'm mean.

Norma There can't be many men who save used tea-bags.

Charles All I ever said was, "It's a pity these things get thrown away".

Norma You say that about everything. Look at that stupid garage. The only thing you haven't got in there is the car. Well you'd better make room for my deep-freeze, I'm warning you.

Charles (*sitting next to her; genuinely*) Oh come on Norma . . . it's my first weekend off in two months. Let's go out and have a bit of fun, eh?

She stares rigidly ahead. He puts an arm along the sofa behind her

Norma? Norm . . .

He puts his face close to hers. She turns to look at him and shudders

Norma Are you wearing a pair of my knickers under that dress?

Charles No I am not.

Norma I wouldn't put it past you. First my ballet tights and now a pair of my knickers. (*She snatches the bottle from him and stands*) Well go to your stupid fancy dress party and I hope it chokes you.

She exits with the bottle

Charles sits miserably as:

> *Susan enters the bedroom from the bathroom carrying her dressing-gown. She is fresh from the bath and wearing a bra and panties. She's towelling wet hair and humming happily to herself. She stands before the mirror, examining herself, particularly her bottom and thighs, both of which she gives a disapproving prod*

> *Charles exits from the living-room as:*

Susan opens the wardrobe door, contemplates, then takes out two dresses. Holds them up against herself, first one and then the other, makes up her mind. But decides she needs a second opinion. She moves towards the door

Susan (*calling*) Keith?

She opens the door. On the landing, right outside the door, is a pair of aluminium step-ladders. The lower half of Keith can be seen, framed in the doorway, up the steps. He remains in this position during the following dialogue. Susan recoils at the sight of the ladder

What are you doing *now*?

Keith Oh . . . hello love . . . I just thought I'd have a quick look for my box while you were getting ready. (*He is totally pre-occupied with the loft*)

Susan I see. (*She closes the bedroom door. Stands a moment, fighting back the desire to go bonkers. Instead, she takes up her cigarettes and sits on the edge of the bed, holding herself tightly in control and then squeezing her eyes closed*) Dear God, I know he tries to do his best for me but couldn't he do it *with* me—just once? (*She moves to open the door and tries to maintain calm*) You see, I walk into the bedroom and two minutes later you're up in the loft. I find that very difficult to live with, Keith. Sorry.

Keith I had it on my mind, you see. Anyway, I'm only half in. Not in at all really, more on the landing than in the loft. I mean, if I was really in the loft you'd be fully-justified . . . (*With a change of tone*) We could make a smashing room up here, y'know.

Susan We're going to the *pictures*.

Keith Plenty of time, it doesn't start till eight.

Susan Oh yes. Sorry. That'll give you time to think about re-tiling the roof. (*She looks at her dress, almost in tears of frustration*)

Keith It's fantastic up here, a whole new world. D'you want to have a look?

She opens the wardrobe, hurls the dress inside

Susan No thank you. I've decided not to go to the pictures, I've decided to go mad instead. You can come if you like. Or perhaps you'd prefer to stay here and think about building an extension to lock me up in. (*She is puffing furiously at her cigarette*)

Keith Do you realize that one sixth of a house is the loft and most people never even set foot in it?

Susan Do you realize that one sixth of the launderette is gents toilet and I've never set foot in that either—d'you think there's something wrong with me, d'you think I'm lacking in the pioneering spirit, d'you think you should never have married me?

Keith Ah yes . . . there it is . . . hang on.

His legs disappear upwards into the loft

Susan I'm trying, but I don't think I can, I think it's going all wrong, d'you know that? (*She sits on the edge of the bed, puffing at her cigarette*)

David enters the kitchen, pursued by Mrs Hinson who holds, with a tea-towel, a hot plate loaded with stodgy food, and her handbag

David (*as he enters*) Will you please stop following me around with a plateful of bloody *food.*

Mrs Hinson You're just like your father—get a meal ready and there he was—gone.

David There is more to life than Meals On Wheels.

Mrs Hinson puts the plate on the table and points at it

Mrs Hinson *Eat.*

David (*keeping the peace*) All right, all right . . . just let me go up and see how she is.

Mrs Hinson (*taking cutlery from a drawer*) She's asleep, I'm telling you. Stop worrying or you'll have a nervous breakdown.

She forces him into the chair. He sighs, then sits and mechanically begins to eat. Mrs Hinson sits and watches him as though he were a child

Keith (*shouting; off*) It's a bit tricky up here . . . ooops!

Susan is suddenly aware of bits of plaster falling on her. She waves a hand at her hair and looks up

Susan The plaster's coming down!

Keith (*off*) You what?

Susan There's a great big crack in the ceiling!

Keith (*off*) There's a what?

Susan Where you're *walking!*

Keith (*off*) What is?

Susan A *crack!*

Keith (*off*) A what?

Susan goes to the door and shouts as though to a child

Susan A—crack. There—is—a—crack—in—the—ceiling—and—it's—all—all—your—fault!

The front doorbell rings

Keith (*off*) A crack? How can there be a crack?

Susan There's somebody at the door which is *also* your fault!

She pulls on her dressing-gown as she exits. In order to get out she has to move the steps to one side, so that both she and the steps move out of sight as:

Charles, still in his Marlene outfit, enters the living-room, followed by Peter

Peter is the same age as Charles but looks younger. He is slim, svelte, "takes care of himself". He too is a doctor. He is wearing an immaculate white suit and is carrying a wide-brimmed black hat. As they enter:

Keith (*shouting; off*) I'm going to bang on the ceiling . . . you tell me when I come to it . . . OK?

Peter Who are you supposed to be?

Charles Marlene Dietrich.

Peter With a moustache, very good.

Charles grits his teeth. He never did like the man

Charles And you?

Peter (*posing*) The Man In The White Suit. There was a film. You remember.

Charles (*of the hat; disdainfully*) What about that thing?

Peter Well I had it in the cupboard so I thought I'd throw it in as a sort of bonus. Some lucky girl gets *me* and the hat. (*He puts it on*) Olé.

Charles scowls

(*Taking off his hat*) Anyway, lets 'em know you've made an effort, eh?

Charles If you want a sherry you'll have to break the bedroom door down —she's got the bottle in there with her.

Peter Ah. You mean . . .

Charles I mean that if we go to this stupid party, it's just you and me. Norma isn't going.

Peter But we don't know anybody.

Charles It did occur to me, yes.

Peter Why isn't she going?

Charles I have no idea.

Peter Ah. I see. (*He knows all about their non-speaking rows*) Why don't *I* have a word with her?

Charles Do what you like.

Peter In the bedroom you say.

Charles, sitting on the sofa, jerks a most unladylike thumb towards the ceiling

Peter exits as:

In the kitchen, David pushes his plate away, scarcely touched

Mrs Hinson Is that all you're going to eat?

David I've had enough. Thank you.

She takes the plate and replaces it with a dessert bowl of pears and a jug of custard from the fridge

Mrs Hinson Well far be it from me, but that's the last decent nourishment you'll be getting. From now on it's back to the frozen wastes of Madam's delights. You should be stocking up.
David I am not a camel.
Mrs Hinson Oh don't be so argumentative, I'm your mother. And eat those pears up, they cost me nearly sixty-five p. Put some of that custard on—you love my custard.

David tips the jug to reveal a solid mass of custard

David When I can dislodge it.
Mrs Hinson You know it won't leave the jug on its own—it's the goodness in it—use your spoon and ease it out.

Hilary enters the kitchen from the hall, wearing a dressing-gown and a rock-hard expression

Hilary (*mock-bright*) I see.
David (*half-standing*) You were asleep.
Hilary Was I?
Mrs Hinson Well the boy's got to eat, hasn't he, he's got to keep his strength up—you don't mind that, dear, surely?

David puts his head in his hands. Hilary offers Mrs Hinson her most regal smile

Hilary Mind? It's like a dream come true. Do finish your picnic. Should I die of hunger during the night, I'll try and do so without disturbing you.
David You're not *eating*.
Hilary I am *now*. (*She seizes the jug of custard, tips the pears into it, takes up a spoon and begins to make her way out*)
Mrs Hinson Actually . . . we were just trying to work out which room he'll be sleeping in. Well, you won't want him in with you, will you dear?

David stands, anguished, wanting to choke her

David Mum, will you please . . .

In the same moment, Hilary, her face changing from disbelief to fury, exits to the hall, and off, we can hear her shouting unformed words of abuse as she chucks things around

Mrs Hinson sits with a prim look on her face. There is a final crash, off

Mrs Hinson I think she's on the turn myself.
David You told me she was asleep!
Mrs Hinson Well how did I know? She looked like she was asleep, I'm not a mind-reader you know.

David exits quickly to the hall

Mrs Hinson remains sitting as;

Peter enters the living-room. He indicates the bottle of sherry he is holding

Peter Well that's it then, all settled.

Keith (*calling; off*) Sue? Susie? Where are you, what are you . . .

Suddenly his legs appear in the bedroom doorway. He drops down to hang framed in the doorway

You've moved the flipping ladder!

Peter (*putting on his hat*) Olé!

Charles scowls at him and moves to get glasses from the cabinet as:

David enters the kitchen. His hair and sweater are splattered with custard

Mrs Hinson Oh yes . . . on the turn she is . . . definitely.

Peter starts to click his fingers and do a Spanish dance as Charles scowls, as Keith swings from the hatch, as Mrs Hinson moves to swab down her beloved David, as the sound of Spanish music is heard, swelling as—

the CURTAIN *falls*

ACT II

The same. Seconds later

Keith is still hanging from the hatch, legs swinging in an attempt to find a foothold

In the living-room, Charles sits on the sofa. He looks irritably at his watch and takes up the yachting magazine to flick at it as:

> *Susan enters the bedroom. She avoids actual physical contact with Keith as she squeezes past and into the room*

Susan (*brusquely*) Excuse me.

She takes off the dressing-gown and puts on a skirt and top as Keith drops to the floor somewhat dramatically and appeals to her

Keith You moved the ladder.
Susan So I did.
Keith You could have broken my legs.
Susan So I could.
Keith I don't understand you, Sue.
Susan No you don't, do you?
Keith What would have happened if I broke both my legs?
Susan You'd get out your soldering iron and think about mending them. (*With a change of tone*) I moved the ladder in order to get out of the room in order to answer the front door.
Keith (*surprised*) We're not expecting anyone.
Susan Neither was Trotsky. (*She pauses*) Your little friend is here . . . (*with a smile*) . . . you'll be delighted to know.
Keith My what?
Susan Katy.
Keith (*staring at the ceiling*) Oh flamin' 'eck.
Susan It's all right, she's not stopping—or so she says—which means she *is* stopping, so if you'd kindly . . .
Keith No I mean that crack: I've just seen it. (*He is still staring up at the ceiling*) Fortunately for you, there's nothing you can do about it, is there? *Is there?*

He makes to put his arms around her but she struggles, unwilling to have him touch her

Keith Give us a kiss.
Susan I don't want a kiss, thank you.
Keith Come on, give us a kiss.

Susan I don't want a kiss. I don't want you to touch me.

A moment. He knows she means it

Keith Katy?
Susan That's right. (*She brushes her hair fiercely*)
Keith Where is she, downstairs?
Susan That's right.
Keith On her own?
Susan That's right.
Keith Where's Gareth?
Susan With "the boys", playing rugby.
Keith (*grinning*) Silly question. (*With a change of tone*) What does she want, did she say?
Susan She wants to see *you*.
Keith Oh come on, don't start all that again.
Susan Why do people have to want anything? Oh I know the only reason *you* ever knock on someone's door is to borrow a drill or tell them they've got smoke coming out of their exhaust but there are people who actually visit just for the sake of visiting. Even visiting boring, overweight, under-the-doctor little housewives like me.
Keith You really are upset, aren't you?
Susan I'm going downstairs.
Keith Because *she's* come?
Susan That's right, it's because *she's* come. We were having such a wonderful time together, you on your hands and knees up there and me down here doing the navigating. It might also occur to you that I'm missing my children.
Keith Sue love . . .
Susan (*coldly*) If you want to drool over Junior Miss Nobody you'd better be quick about it—five minutes and she's out.

Susan exits from the bedroom

Peter enters the living-room, cheerfully rubbing his hands together as;

Keith sits glumly on the edge of the bed

Peter (*meaning Norma*) Five minutes.
Keith (*suddenly realizing*) Waddaya mean . . . under the doctor?

Keith exits from the bedroom as:

Peter closes the living-room door and in doing so, becomes aware of the crack in the wall

Peter (*indicating*) Is this a crack?
Charles (*not looking*) That's right, it's a crack.
Peter Thought so. (*He peers closer*) What—settlement?
Charles No, no, we had an earthquake, I'm surprised you didn't read about it.

Peter looks at him for a moment. Then:

Peter Ha!

Charles tosses down the magazine as Peter glances at his watch, whistles cheerfully under his breath, does a little more of his fandango

Charles Have you got thyroid trouble or something?

Peter I'm happy: I'm going to a party.

Charles That makes you happy, does it?

Peter Of course, you need alcohol to get you into the spirit of things, don't you? *(He pours himself a sherry, and one for Charles)*

Charles Do I.

Peter Oh you do you know you do. Sad in a way. I drink, of course I drink. Well you know I do. But I must say there have been times when not one single drop of the stuff has passed my lips and still I've been the life and soul. Mind you. Supply and demand, laugh clown laugh, all that sort of rubbish.

Charles You do realize that the chances are she won't speak to me for the rest of the evening.

Peter That's the impression I got, yes.

Charles What did she say?

Peter More or less word for word what you just said.

Charles She actually said she wasn't going to speak to me.

Peter I believe she intends employing yours truly as a sort of interpreter.

Charles *(sighing)* Sometimes I wish I was on a desert island.

Peter D'you know anyone who's going to be there? *(He mimes dancing with a partner)*

Charles What? Not a soul, it's all down to Norma.

Peter I'm wondering about the ladies.

Charles Be next to the gents, I shouldn't wonder. *(He smirks, rather pleased with his joke)*

Peter The ladies.

Charles I thought you were bringing someone.

Peter I was. Her husband came back from Zimbabwe or she had to wash her hair, something like that, I can't remember.

Charles notices that one of his shoelaces is undone. He stands, puts the shoe on the coffee table to tie the lace

Charles I didn't start all this, you know: she did.

Peter I've got this feeling I'm really going to click tonight. I might even propose to someone. The thing is, you see, I suddenly feel the need to get married again.

Charles I mean. Look at me. *(He faces Peter)* Have I or have I not made a bloody fine effort?

Peter Bloody fine. Who are you again?

Charles *(through gritted teeth)* Marlene Dietrich.

Peter Are you sure?

Charles Now look here, *chum* . . .

Peter Can I ask you something personal?

Charles No I am not wearing knickers.

Peter What I meant was . . . (*he extends his arms*) . . . can I book the last waltz now or will I have to stand in line with all the others?

Charles (*moving away to sit in the chair*) Stupid bloody idea . . . who's ever heard of a fancy dress party?

Peter Last fancy dress party I went to . . . chap turned up in a coffin.

Charles How can you turn up to a party in a coffin?

Peter They delivered him in a small lorry. Carried him through, propped him up in a corner on the patio.

Charles Colder outside, was it?

Peter squats on the arm of the sofa near Charles

Peter Barbecue affair, lights in the trees, that sort of thing.

Charles A coffin?

Peter As I live and breathe.

Charles What was he supposed to be?

Peter Dead I think. No-one actually had the nerve to ask him.

Charles Well if no-one actually asked him, perhaps he *was*. Did his eyes move or anything?

Peter Oh yes. Quite often. Mind you, he never spoke. Just leaned there at a rakish thirty-five degrees knocking back gins and tonic. And dropping peanuts all down his pyjamas. White silk they were—with a Union Jack embroidered on the pocket. Interesting touch that, I thought. "I died for Britain" sort of thing. *But*—and this is the really creepy part —it was only after they'd carried him out and loaded him back on to the lorry that we realized that nobody actually knew him. Not the host, nobody. So. You never know, he could be there tonight. (*He gets up and moves back to the sherry*)

Charles Look. What about *Norma*?

Peter What about her?

Charles Is she coming or isn't she?

Peter Don't—worry.

Charles Because if I've done all this for nothing. (*He crosses his legs irritably, revealing an expanse of white flesh over shoe and sock*)

Peter Tell you something, Chas . . . you've got a damned good pair of legs. I've noticed that about men: when they put on a skirt, more often than not they've got a bloody good pair of legs.

Charles Have they, have they really.

Norma enters, gaily. She wears a black dress, a black lace shawl on her head, a flower in her hair, and carries a black fan

Now look here Norma, are we going or aren't we?

She looks at him as if he's something alien and turns her beam on Peter

Norma I'd love a glass of sherry before we go.

Peter (*pouring sherry*) You look wonderful. Super. The bees' knees. (*He puts the bottle back inside the cabinet and hands Norma her drink*)

Norma Thank you.

Charles Would someone mind telling me what she's supposed to be? (*He

dips into his evening bag to produce his pipe and fills the pipe from his
pouch which is inside the bag)
Norma I love your suit.
Peter Yes, *I* do.
Charles What *is* she?
Norma (*to Peter*) I thought I'd go as a Spanish contessa.
Peter Ah! Well there we are, you see—I'm a count.
Charles Five minutes ago you were The Man In The White Suit And
The Stupid Black Hat.
Peter That's the thing though today, isn't it—adaptability.
Norma How clever of you to see us as a pair.
Peter Trio though really, isn't it?
Norma Is there someone else?
Charles Don't push me beyond my limits, Norma. (*He angrily raps his*
pipe on his shoe)
Peter We must consider Charles.
Norma Why must we?
Peter For the same reason we shin up a mountain I suppose. Now let's
see . . . if I'm a Spanish count and you're my contessa . . . Charles can
be . . . got it!
Norma A sherpa.
Peter Charles can be my mother-in-law! They've always got a mother-in-
law, these Spaniards . . . they walk about three feet behind and scowl
over a dark moustache so apart from the brogues you're spot on, Chas.
(*He bends closer to Charles*) That's only if someone asks if we're a sort
of tableau. Other than that, you're a free agent.

Mrs Hinson enters the kitchen, still in her pinnie and dabbing at David's
sweater with a sponge. She moves to the sink and continues dabbing as:

Charles (*seeking dignity*) Norma, are we speaking or aren't we? I shan't
ask you again.
Norma (*to Peter*) Did you notice my new tree?
Peter Oh it's a *tree*. (*With a change of tone*) Very nice. Goes awfully well
with the pond.
Charles (*growling*) Bloody pond.
Norma What time do you think we should leave?
Peter Where is it again?
Norma Hampton Wick-ish.
Peter Oh—what—half an hour?
Charles (*standing*) All right! I'm not going.
Peter Sorry?
Charles I said I am not going. Play your silly games, the pair of you, I'm
staying here.
Norma (*cupping an ear*) Do I hear the distant rumble of yet another sulk?
Charles I am not walking to that car dressed like this with you two
dressed like that and that is final.
Norma (*moving to smile sweetly at him*) Will you please stop sulking and
face the fact that due to your totally insensitive behaviour I am not

talking to you. Now pull yourself together, freshen up your lipstick and we'll be on our way.

Charles (*moving to the door*) I am not going. Not going. Not—going. Not —*going*!

Charles exits, closing the door behind him

Norma You know the real trouble, don't you? (*She opens the door*) His heart was set on Batman.

Norma exits from the living-room as:

Charles enters the bedroom. Now minus the wig and carrying a yachting magazine. He lies on the bed and reads as:

Peter gives a shrug, sits on the arm of the sofa, and sips his sherry as:

David enters the kitchen from the hall

Mrs Hinson Well?
David She's crying.
Mrs Hinson Because she made a fool of herself I suppose.
David No, because she went to kick me and stubbed her toe on the door.
Mrs Hinson She can be very *violent*, can't she son?
David She gets—upset.
Mrs Hinson Your Auntie Florrie used to get violent. (*She glances out of the window at the sky*) It depended where the moon was.
David Yes, all right Mum—and she didn't make a fool of herself, she was entitled to get upset—all right?

He looks at her pointedly. By way of answer, she holds up his sweater

Mrs Hinson There.
David Very nice. Thank you. (*He pulls on the sweater*)
Mrs Hinson That's all right, boy. Now where was I . . . oh yes . . . (*She bends, under strain, to open the cupboard under the sink*)
David (*anxiously*) What are you looking for?

But she is straightening up, holding the plant

Mrs Hinson What's my plant doing in here?
David Trying—to get some *sleep.* (*He takes the plant from her, shoves it back into the cupboard and shuts the door*) What—are you *looking* for?
Mrs Hinson The washing powder.
David The what?
Mrs Hinson You've moved it again, haven't you, no wonder my nerves are bad.
David No, you moved it like you move everything else and I put it back where it belongs and you're not washing at this time of night thankyou-verymuch.
Mrs Hinson Was it Daz or Ariel?
David How do I know? . . . Bold.
Mrs Hinson Oh yes I think you're right. I always use Persil myself—Persil

and elbow-grease, but there's no accounting nowadays, is there—see if you can find it for me, will you son, I go quite breathless when I bend of late. (*She sits wearily*)
David (*patiently*) Why . . . why . . . do you want the washing powder?
Mrs Hinson Because we might win a prize.
David A what?
Mrs Hinson I *saw* him.
David *Who?*
Mrs Hinson The chap on the telly—him in the white suit.

In the living-room, Peter looks at his watch, stands and impatiently paces a little as:

David What d'you mean, you saw him?
Mrs Hinson He was going into the house opposite. He'll be doing his rounds, I shouldn't wonder, up that side and down this. Course, what your father would have done was nip out and get a selection.

Peter exits from the living-room, taking his hat with him

David Mum . . . listen to me . . . please.

He sits opposite her. She knows what he's going to say

I'm taking you home. It's my fault, my fault, I should have taken you before she got back. I'm very sorry, Mum, but that's how it is, no arguments.
Mrs Hinson Yes, that's all right, David, I quite understand.
David (*taking her hand*) You can see how things are.
Mrs Hinson It's just a peculiar feeling, that's all—being jettisoned by your own flesh and blood.
David It isn't like that and you know it.
Mrs Hinson (*doing her close-to-tears bit*) If your poor dear father could hear the way you've just spoken to me.
David You're doing it *again*.
Mrs Hinson Excuse me. (*She stands and takes off her pinnie and folds it neatly over the chair*)
David (*sighing*) Mum—please.
Mrs Hinson Excuse me, I want to get my things together. And you needn't take me in the car, there's bound to be a train. Sooner or later. And I can always get a bus from the station.
David You don't have to go *now*.
Mrs Hinson Oh but excuse me you just told me to.
David I didn't mean *right now*.
Mrs Hinson Oh I think you did, son. Although I like to believe you were acting under orders.
David (*taking her limp hand*) I didn't mean right now—all right?
Mrs Hinson Well when did you mean?
David (*losing ground*) Well . . . when you're ready.
Mrs Hinson Well if I go now I shall miss my programme and I'm sure even she wouldn't wish that on me.

David No Mum.

Mrs Hinson God only knows I don't get many pleasures since your poor dear father passed on.

David Watch your programme and then I'll take you home.

Mrs Hinson Yes, that's all right then, son, I'm not one to stay where I'm not wanted, never have been. I'll just go and watch my programme out of everybody's way and then you can take me home in the morning.

David In the *morning*?

Mrs Hinson That'll be best, when you're nice and fresh and the roads are dry. (*She even manages a dry little kiss on his cheek*) You're a good boy David, I don't know why they can't leave you in peace, really I don't. (*She makes to go*) I wish you'd get the *TV Times* though: they don't tell you half what you want to know in the paper.

Mrs Hinson exits to the hall, clutching her handbag

David, left alone and defeated again, slumps into a chair at the table as:

Susan enters the living-room. She is carrying her cigarettes and matches and a paper bag containing a box of chocolates. She sits on the sofa, edgier than ever, and puts the chocolates on the coffee table as:

Keith and Katy enter the living-room. Katy is a little younger than Susan. Slim and attractive and with a worrying brightness about her. She and Keith once had a ding-dong and she's still somewhat fulsome with him

At the same time, David stands. He's suddenly remembered the plant which he takes out of the cupboard and stands with it, looking around desperately trying to think what to do with it as:

Katy (*as they enter*) I love the kitchen: all those super cupboards.

Keith I've got some great ideas for that kitchen, really great.

Katy *Super.*

David exits from the kitchen into the garage with the plant as:

Keith examines the contents of the drinks cabinet

Keith Now then . . . er . . . there's some sherry or a tin of lager. (*He holds up the sherry bottle and squints at its contents*)

Katy Sherry would be super: just a tiny one. (*She indicates how tiny with finger and thumb*)

Keith Sue?

Susan smiles and indicates a massive one with finger and thumb. Katy suddenly swirls around

Katy This is a super room: really nice.

Keith Not yet it isn't.

Katy When it's finished I mean. I can just see it in the summer.

Keith I've got some terrific ideas for this room, really terrific.

Susan He'll be starting on it just as soon as he's finished the sidecar. It's a question of priorities.

Katy You'll do wonders I know you will.

Susan Oh goodie.

Katy Well then . . . (*she raises her glass*) . . . here's to the new house and my favourite couple, I love you dearly and I know you'll be very happy here because I get the vibes—really super super vibes, you know? So here's to you and your really super, super happiness.

She knocks back the sherry in one gulp and thrusts the glass at Keith for a refill and then swirls around the room, beaming rather bravely as Keith and Susan look at each other

So . . .you've got the entire house to yourselves.

Susan More or less.

Katy Sorry—drink this and away.

Keith How's old Gareth?

Katy They're playing at home today so I should think at this very minute he's having a lovely time distending his bladder and throwing pint glasses into the Thames. (*She stops swirling to regard the crack above the door*)

Keith That's where I'm going to have my display, on that wall.

Susan Lots and lots of little men on motor bikes disappearing in strict formation down the crack.

Keith There won't be a crack. (*Behind Katy's back, he mouths at Susan, "Stop picking on me"*)

Katy Have you still *got* your motor bike?

Keith Not the Triumph: I swopped it for a beautiful old Beeza.

Katy Beeza?

Keith B.S.A.

Susan (*sweetly*) Bloody Sore Arse.

Katy Oops, sorry, should've remembered, change the subject. (*She sits next to Susan*) Of course, a lot of people don't like this sort of house but I think they're fun.

Susan Oh goodie.

Katy Don't you?

Susan Oh yes. Every night I go to bed and close my eyes and think, "Isn't this house fun?" and sometimes I can't stop laughing.

Keith Hello, what's this? (*He's noticed the chocolates*)

Susan Katy brought me some chocolates, isn't that *super*?

Keith You're on a diet.

Susan I did mention it.

Katy Trust me to do the wrong thing.

Keith She's got a fantastic body, hasn't she, Katy?

Katy Sue? I mean, *twins* and everything . . . *super*.

Keith There you are you see: she thinks she's fat.

Susan (*grittily*) Overweight.

Katy Sue? Fat?

Keith Don't you?

Susan Overweight, slightly overweight.

Keith Truth is, she'd like to be as skinny as you are.

Katy Christ, I'd like to put some on. I mean, Christ, really, I'd love to have your sort of shape. Really.
Keith Something to get hold of—right?
Katy (*to Keith, with a sexy edge*) Typical male. (*To both of them*) But if you really want to lose weight . . . I mean, really . . . there's only one way to do it . . . (*Brightly*) Worry. Worry, worry, worry. Worry, worry, worry, worry, worry. (*She beams at them*)

A moment

Susan Well I'm sorry we've got to go out.
Katy Somewhere exciting?
Keith Pictures then a meal. (*Instantly he remembers he's forgotten to book the table*)
Katy Lovely.
Susan What time did you book the table?
Keith Bloody 'ell.
Susan I don't believe it.
Keith I'll do it now.
Susan I asked you to do it this afternoon.
Keith I can't do *everything*.

They glare at each other. Katy studiously smokes her cigarette. Keith digs into his pocket for change

Susan You can phone my mother while you're there, see how they are.
Keith Yes.
Susan Make sure you send them my love.
Keith I'll send them a photograph if you like—I mean, they've been gone nearly twenty-four hours, they might have forgotten what you look like . . . Right, I'm off, see you Kate, come again . . .

He bends and almost kisses her, then realizes what he is doing, and exits

Katy All that energy. He doesn't change, does he?
Susan Not often, no.
Katy He does so *much*.
Susan Mmmm . . . *and* he's thinking of joining the Open University.
Katy Is he really?
Susan *Mmmm* . . . he's taking a Ph.D. in Good Intentions.
Katy Can I see upstairs?
Susan Why not?

They exit from the living-room as:

Peter enters the bedroom from the landing

Peter Oh come on, you're as bad as each other, always have been.
Charles What d'you mean, as bad as each other?
Peter (*admiring himself in the mirror*) It's a funny thing that, isn't it? You'd think we'd get to middle age and chuck out all the counter-productive emotions, shed 'em like an old skin . . . instead of which it's more peaks and bloody troughs than you ever knew existed.

Charles What do you mean, as bad as each other?

Peter I mean you sulk.

Charles Who does?

Peter You do. Both of you. You have a row and you sulk.

Charles I do not sulk. I withdraw. (*He goes back to his magazine*)

Peter takes out a comb and runs it through his hair as he drifts idly into the bathroom as:

Susan and Katy enter the living-room

Katy (*as they enter*) It really is, it's *super*.

They sit on the sofa

Will they be all right on their own?

Susan They're not on their own, they're with my mother.

Katy Yes of course they are. (*After a slight pause*) I expect you're worried though.

Susan Not worried, no.

Katy No, not worried—concerned. You were so clever giving up everything to have a family.

Susan Yes I was, wasn't I? I wonder what Keith gave up? What *do* they give up?

Katy Gareth gave up training once a week. Well at the beginning anyway.

Susan Oh yes—Keith gave up opening the car door.

Katy It was terribly brave of you to have twins.

Susan Just a question of pushing twice as hard, really. But then you don't get anything in this world without pushing, do you?

Katy What I mean is, getting the whole family over and done with in one go.

Susan You think two is enough.

Katy Don't you?

Susan I sometimes think I'd like ten.

Katy Wow!

Susan Twelve, eighteen, twenty-four, a hundred and thirty-nine.

Katy That's what I've always envied about you. You've always known exactly what you wanted. (*Sighing*) You're so lucky, you and Keith.

Susan You had him before I did—if you'd played your cards right it could've been you riding shotgun.

Katy (*suddenly very serious*) I think . . . I think perhaps there's something wrong with me . . . *vis-à-vis* a normal one-to-one situation.

Susan Sex you mean.

Katy No, not sex, sex is super.

Susan Is it, I can't remember.

Katy No . . . what I mean is . . . I wasn't just passing when I knocked on your door.

Susan (*dreading it*) No?

Katy I wanted you to know before anyone else tells you and gets it all wrong. He's left me. Gareth. He's gone.

A moment. Then Susan gets up and replenishes their glasses

Susan When you say "left" . . .

Katy Oh it's permanent. He's taken his book. And his undies. There's someone else. He wants to marry her.

Susan When was all this?

Katy Two weeks ago. I would have told you then but I was under sedation. And the stomach pump and everything. You know. The pills.

Susan Oh.

Katy I've got a terrible feeling I've ruined your evening.

Susan In a way . . . I'm not sure . . . but I think . . . I think I've given up on this evening.

They sit side by side gulping their sherry

Katy It's all right though. I saw the solicitor yesterday afternoon and somehow that sort of did it for me. I've thought it right through from end to end and I can see Gareth had a point. I'm awful.

Susan No. Not *really*. Not *awful*.

Katy I'm all right though. Truly. I've come to terms with myself, I have really, I'm fine. Super. Absolutely one hundred percent together.

Suddenly she is howling with tears and clinging to Susan who puts comforting arms around her

Keith enters

Keith (*as he enters*) The only time they can do us is nine o'clock so we'll have to miss the film and settle for the midnight movie, waddaya think?

Susan points wildly at Katy. He misconstrues

Pity old Gareth isn't here, we could've made up a foursome.

With a loud cry, Katy exits, sobbing

Keith, bewildered, looks at Susan

Susan shoves her glass into his hand and exits after Katy, as:

Peter enters the bedroom from the bathroom

Peter Things a bit dodgy, are they?

Charles Don't—fish.

Keith exits from the living-room, taking the glass and the chocolates

Peter I wouldn't worry: women generally go a bit funny when they move house.

Charles Do they.

Peter Oh yes. Although come to think of it, women generally go a bit funny full stop.

Charles How would you know? You've never been with one long enough to find out. (*He resumes staring at his magazine*)

Peter throws up his hands in mock-surrender and exits to the landing as:

Hilary enters the kitchen, in a dressing-gown, carrying a plate piled high with one of Mrs Hinson's stodgy delights. She sees the dreaded pinnie, holds it up momentarily, then makes to tip the food into the wastebin— but finds it full. She exits into the garage with the bin and plate as:

David and Mrs Hinson enter the living-room

David What d'you mean, it won't work?

Mrs Hinson (*pointing at the television*) Nothing *happens.*

He sighs heavily and gets on his hands and knees trying to make the set work as Mrs Hinson sits impatiently on the sofa, handbag on her lap

Hilary enters the kitchen with the remains of "her" plant arrangement. She moves straight across and exits into the hallway

Mrs Hinson Can't you phone the engineer?

David No.

Mrs Hinson That's what they're paid for, go on, phone the engineer.

David Who's been messing about with it, that's what I want to know.

Mrs Hinson I hope you're not accusing *me*, my son.

Hilary enters the living-room with the plant and moves straight to bend over David

Hilary (*sweetly*) Why is she still here?

David (*fiddling with the set*) Her name is "my mother" and she's here because she wants to watch her stupid bloody quiz programme. (*But he sees the plant and is immediately guilty*) What are you doing with that?

Hilary (*still sweetly*) It was in the dustbin . . . now who would want to put my plant in the dustbin? (*She turns and beams at Mrs Hinson*)

Mrs Hinson *Hello* dear . . . (*she sees the plant*) . . . been admiring my arrangement, have you? (*With her prim smile*) David's little thank-you present to his mother.

Hilary beams at her and exits with the plant

David (*shouting desperately after her*) There's one each . . . one *each*!

Mrs Hinson Your father would have phoned the engineer.

Hilary bursts into the kitchen. She bangs the plant down on the table and looks around to find something on which to vent her fury. She sees Mrs Hinson's pinnie, snatches it up, tries to rip it apart, as a last resort, putting one end between her teeth for better leverage. Finally she gives up and hurls the pinnie outside into the garage, snatches up the plant and hurls that after it. Her rage sated, she slumps into a chair

He was very good like that, your father. The merest hint of trouble and he was straight on to the relevant authority. He had a wonderful nose for that sort of thing. I think it was due to his mother being half-Irish.

Hilary exits from the kitchen into the hall

Your Rosemary was good with televisions, I seem to remember. What she used to do was twiddle with those knobs at the back.

Hilary enters the living-room, beaming at Mrs Hinson

Feeling better, are we?

Hilary Much better, thank you.

At the sound of her voice, David—who has been on his hands and knees with his eyes to heaven—starts fiddling with the television again

Oh dear, trouble with the telly?

Mrs Hinson I keep telling him, he should phone the engineer.

Hilary Or Rosemary . . . why don't you phone Rosemary, darling?

David Who's been messing about with it?

Hilary I hope you're not accusing your mother . . . (*moving closer to him, but still smiling*) . . . besides which, I thought we were supposed to be going *out*.

David I thought you were supposed to be *ill*.

Mrs Hinson I tell you what, Hilary.

Hilary (*beaming*) What's that, David's Mother?

Mrs Hinson I can't see that picture I gave you. That "Donkey with the Straw Hat". Or was it a bicycle?

Hilary I think it was both, actually.

Mrs Hinson That's a real painting, you know, not one of those whatsits. I thought you would have liked it, being artistic.

Hilary Can you see any other pictures in this room? No. That's because we haven't got them out yet, any of them.

Mrs Hinson That would have gone lovely with your three-piece suite, that picture.

Hilary If you look *really* closely . . . you'll notice that the three-piece suite isn't here either . . . (*She beams but turns to David*) I want her out of here, do I make myself clear?

David Shut up. Both of you—shut up!

Mrs Hinson Oo-er, temper, temper.

Hilary moves away to sit, biting a nail and staring at Mrs Hinson with bubbling hatred

David It's no good, I think the tube must have gone.

Mrs Hinson Well can't you find another one?

David turns on her, leaning over her with wild eyes, just about controlling himself

David No. No I can't.

Mrs Hinson Well it's no good standing there popping your eyes out at me, look at the time.

David You'll have to miss it for once, won't you?

Mrs Hinson I knew I shouldn't have stayed here.

David You're right, you're absolutely right, get your coat, I'm taking you home.

Mrs Hinson Too late for that now, it's coming up to the commercials.

Hilary (*shocked*) Don't argue, Mum—*please*—David's indecision is *final*.

David OK, that's it . . . the pair of you . . . that is it! (*He makes to go out,* *but leans over Hilary)* Twenty-six people I look after in that office . . . twenty-six happy, smiling, contented people. But *here—you two* . . . *(He moves away and, generally)* You're right. I'm weak, I'm useless, I give up. I give—*up! (He moves to the door)*

Mrs Hinson Where are you going?

David For a walk.

He exits

Mrs Hinson *(calling after him)* You should have two televisions, man in your position!

The front door slams off. Hilary moves to look through the "window", seething

Walking around, this time of night, he'll get himself mugged.

Hilary He won't go far: down to the off-licence I should think. *(She turns and beams)* It's about as far as the cord will stretch.

Mrs Hinson does her whining, close-to-tears bit

Mrs Hinson He knows how I look forward to my programme.

Hilary turns on her, a manic gleam in her eye

Hilary And you deserve to see it.

Mrs Hinson I *do*.

Hilary Right! Follow me!

She levers Mrs Hinson from the chair and Mrs Hinson resists, clutching her handbag as though from a thief

Mrs Hinson Where are we going?

Hilary You want to see your programme . . . right . . . I'll make sure you see it . . . I owe it to you . . .

She shoves the protesting Mrs Hinson towards the door

Mrs Hinson Where are we going, where are we going?

Hilary *(shoving her)* You want to see your programme, you shall *see* your programme . . .

They exit from the living-room as:

Susan enters the kitchen. She takes out the tin of biscuits and sits at the table, eating one of the biscuits as:

A front doorbell rings

A moment later, Peter puts his head round the bedroom door and comes in

Charles ignores him, studiously reading his magazine

Peter Oh come on Charles.

Charles Will you please go away and inform my wife that moving was *her* idea, I was quite happy where I was, thankyouverymuch.

Peter Yes, I must say it's awfully brave, moving at your age. I thought the next move would be the cottage in the country.

Charles (*gritting his teeth*) Labour-saving devices . . . I *hate* labour-saving devices . . . I like to see *Norma* working. (*Frowning*) Who was that at the door?

Peter I dunno: I was on my way up to woo you. Some woman in a dressing-gown.

Charles Is *everyone* going to this rotten party—what's she doing down there, running a recruiting campaign? Why does she have to *organize* all the time?

Peter Come on, on your feet.

Charles I'm reading.

Norma enters the bedroom from the landing

Charles ignores her. She has a card up her sleeve if he did but know it

Norma Well?

Peter (*shrugging*) You try. I'm popping down the road for a cigar. (*He moves to door*) To go with the hat.

Charles Why don't you get a gold tooth while you're about it?

Peter beams, unoffended, and exits to the landing

Norma You're not coming.

Charles No.

Norma I may take that as definite.

Charles You may.

Norma You don't mind if Peter and I go.

Charles Have fun.

Norma And you'll stay here on your own.

Charles Absolutely.

Norma Not quite: I've found some company for you.

She beams, and exits, beckoning for him to follow with a playfully crooked finger

Charles Company?

He exits from the bedroom as:

Hilary, still in dressing-gown, pushes Mrs Hinson into the living-room. Mrs Hinson is clutching her handbag. Hilary gets her across and seated in the chair where she remains with hands on bag, knees and ankles together, staring hatefully at Hilary who points exaggeratedly at the television as: Norma—still beaming—graciously leads Charles in by the hand. He is still in drag and wigless

Norma Hello again.

She seats Charles in the sofa

This is my husband . . . he'll be delighted to watch television with you, won't you Charles?

Mrs Hinson (*shyly*) How-do.

Charles stares at her, open-mouthed. Hilary is staring at Charles, but manages:

Hilary It really is very kind of you.
Norma Not at all.
Hilary Well if you'll excuse me . . .
Norma Of course.

Hilary and Norma move towards the door

Hilary And thank you again.
Norma Isn't that what neighbours are for?

Hilary and Norma exit

A moment between Mrs Hinson and Charles who can't take his eyes off her. She finally points to the television

Mrs Hinson I notice you've got a twenty-six inch.

Charles stares at Mrs Hinson who stares at the television as:

Katy enters the bedroom from the bathroom. She is dabbing her eyes and arranges herself dramatically on the bed as:

Keith enters the kitchen from the hall

Keith D'you think I should cancel the table?
Susan If you hadn't been messing about in the loft we would have gone ages ago.
Keith No we wouldn't.
Susan I say we would.
Keith Keep your voice down.
Susan Oh shut up.
Keith What's got into you?
Susan Just about everything if you really want to know . . . you *and* her *and* her skinny legs *and* her rotten box of chocolates . . . my God, chocolates, how calculating can you get? (*She sorts out another biscuit*)
Keith I didn't ask her to come.
Susan I'm beginning to wonder.
Keith Don't be daft, woman.
Susan Get rid of her.

Keith exits from the kitchen to the hall

Susan sits at the table, eating biscuits, as:

Norma enters the living-room carrying her black shawl and Peter's hat

Charles is still staring at Mrs Hinson

Norma Well now . . . is everybody happy?
Charles Who *is* she?
Norma (*loving his horror*) Her name is Mrs Hinson and you'll get on terribly well together I know you will.
Mrs Hinson I'll tell you what, dear . . . (*she levers herself from the chair*)

... I'll just use your toilet before I settle.

Norma I'll show you where it is.

Mrs Hinson I know where it is, thank you. They're all the same these houses. Like boxes.

Mrs Hinson exits

Norma puts her shawl over the back of the chair and Peter's hat on the seat of the chair

Charles What is she *doing* here?

Norma It's an emergency. (*She turns on the television and beams at him*) Unless she watches her programme, she gets withdrawal symptoms. (*She moves closer to him and, conspiratorially*) This is the lady who did such a splendid job on the doorstep across the way. I want you to be very nice to her: she may have a friend of similar persuasion.

She taps her nose as though warning him to be a good boy and exits

Charles stares at the television, trying to work out what is happening as:

Keith enters the bedroom, putting his head round the door and then entering quietly

Keith (*whispering*) Are you asleep?

Katy I was but it doesn't matter.

Keith Oh. Are you feeling better?

Katy I get this terrible pressure in my neck and I feel I'm going to faint.

Keith Oh dear. You won't be staying long, will you?

Katy Don't bully me, Keith ... I realize now I've been bullied all my adult life.

Keith's eyes wander to the ceiling

Keith Will you excuse me a minute? (*He stands on the bed to stare up at the ceiling*)

Katy She's never really liked me, has she?

Keith (*preoccupied*) No.

Katy Not since Ivan's party and that door getting stuck.

He gets down and talks close to her

Keith Will you do something for me?

She takes his arm, misconstruing

Katy You know I will.

Keith I want you to lie here, nice and quiet, while I go up and have another look.

Katy Up where?

Keith Up there. If it happens in the middle of the night, we've had it. (*He moves on to the landing and sets the step-ladder in position in the doorway*)

Katy (*apprehensively*) Shouldn't Susan be here?

He puts a finger to lips and climbs the steps

Keith Give us a shout if anything looks like shifting.

He goes out of sight as:

Susan exits from the kitchen as:

Mrs Hinson enters the living-room

Mrs Hinson (*as she enters*) I say, have you got the *TV Times*, I want to read my article. (*She positions herself straightaway in the chair for her night's viewing, hands folded neatly across her bag and totally unselfconscious about being in someone else's home. She's also sitting on Peter's hat if she did but know it. Her eyes seldom wander from the television*)
Charles Sorry. I can offer you *The Yachting World* or *The Lancet*.
Mrs Hinson No thanks all the same I'm not keen on dancing, never have been to be quite honest.

She stares at the television. Charles stares at her as, in the bedroom:

Katy (*coming to the end of a long story*) Anyway, he says he loves her so who am I to stand in his way? I don't know who she is, this woman, but apparently she's got red hair and plays the piano in *The Black Lion*. (*But suddenly she is sitting bolt upright as though from a nightmare*) Where are you? Why have you left me on my own? Please don't leave me! (*She sobs and wails "Don't leave me on my own" and thrashes the pillows*)
Keith (*off*) What's going on, what's happening?

Susan hurries into the bedroom, shoving the ladder out of the way, to comfort the sobbing Katy

Susan There, there, it's all right, it's all right, Susie's here, Susie's here . . . (*As she would comfort a child wakened by a nightmare*)

With a yell, Keith comes through the hatch and crashes on to the landing

At the sound of his yell, Katy sobs louder and runs into the bathroom, slamming the door behind her

Keith hops about on the landing, clutching his injured ankle. (From now on, he will walk with an exaggerated limp.) Susan, irritated beyond belief by him, slams the bedroom door in his face and moves to sit on the bed and stare at the bathroom door from behind which can be heard the sound of Katy's dramatic sobbing as:

Norma enters the living-room with a bowl of nuts which she offers to Mrs Hinson who regards them with deep suspicion

Mrs Hinson What are these supposed to be?
Norma Pistachios. Do have one.
Mrs Hinson Yes, but what are they?
Norma They're a form of nut.
Mrs Hinson Not if they're nuts, no. The thing is, I've got no mastication. My sister's just the same. Her teeth went immediately prior to her hubby.

Norma Oh dear.

Keith dashes into the kitchen from the hall. He grabs a glass which he quickly fills with water and dashes out again as:

Mrs Hinson He doesn't say much, does he, your hubbie?

Norma Charles is one of the great after-dinner listeners, aren't you darling?

Mrs Hinson Oo-er. My David's executive.

Norma, beaming, offers Charles a nut. He ignores it, stares at Mrs Hinson. Norma perches on the arm of the sofa, delicately selecting a nut, as:

In the bedroom, Susan sits on the bed facing the closed bathroom door. From inside the bathroom, Katy's hysterical sobbing can be heard

Keith hurriedly limps in with the glass of water

Keith Give her this.

Susan What is it?

Keith Water.

Susan Water's not going to do any good, is it—listen to her.

Keith Christ . . . my razor's in there.

Susan So is mine . . . (*she takes the glass from him*) . . . go and phone the doctor.

Keith I don't *know* her doctor.

Susan *Our* doctor.

Keith They're never in—not the weekend—they're always out yachting.

Susan Go and phone the doctor. Now. Go and phone the doctor. *Now.*

Her look is enough to galvanize him into action. He starts digging into a pocket for change

You don't need money, go next door, they've got a phone, tell them it's an emergency.

Keith Good idea.

Keith hurriedly limps out

Susan takes a bottle of pills from a drawer. As she unscrews the top, there is a burst of wailing from Katy

Susan (*cynically*) Mummy's here . . . Mummy's here . . .

She moves towards the bathroom. But Katy's wailing grows louder. Susan looks at the pills, then, as she knocks one back with the glass of water:

In the living-room:

Mrs Hinson Who did you say you were again?

Charles (*stiffly*) Marlene Dietrich.

Norma *En passant.*

Mrs Hinson Marlene Dietrich didn't have a moustache. Not in *The Blue Angel* she didn't. She had a top hat though, definitely—and her hair was longer.

Peter enters the living-room, cheerily, a long thin cigar clenched between his teeth as:

Susan exits from the bedroom

Peter Right then, who's for the off?
Charles (*unable to resist*) I wear—a wig.
Mrs Hinson That's all right dear, a lot of people do nowadays.

But Peter has come into her line of vision and she sees him and is ecstatic, pointing at him

It's him . . . I said it was him.

Peter is decidedly self-conscious under her adoring gaze and removes his cigar

Peter Good-evening.
Mrs Hinson I knew I was right, I told my son, I said to my David, "It's him," I said. You are you, aren't you?
Peter Er . . .
Norma His name is Peter and he's a Spanish count.
Peter (*striking a half-hearted pose*) Olé.
Mrs Hinson And there's me thinking he was Bold.
Charles More—shifty, I'd say.
Mrs Hinson We did though: we thought you was either Bold or Ariel.
Peter Well I never.
Mrs Hinson Or Persil. (*In her confidential tone, eyes fixed firmly on the television*) She can't wash a thing, you know—you-know-who. I've never been a one to talk, but her washing isn't a patch on his previous. She was a funny girl that Rosemary but I'll give her this, she could wash a shirt. Mind you, her ironing wasn't up to much. I think where she was brought up it was all gas.

The others are mesmerized

Norma (*to Charles*) You're definitely not coming.
Charles I would have thought you'd seen to that. (*He glares at Mrs Hinson*)
Mrs Hinson (*eyes glued*) D'you mind being quiet please, it's starting.

The others speak sotto voce despite themselves

Charles Oh my God! I could understand if it was *Mastermind* . . . but *him*. (*He gestures angrily at the television*)
Peter Right, give me your keys, I'll drive there, you drive back, fair enough?
Norma I thought we were going in your car?

Charles smirks at their argument and settles into the sofa to watch the television

Peter (*how could she think that?*) I came by cab.
Norma But we said we were going in your car.

Peter We can go in yours, can't we? I'll drive.
Norma Not my car you won't, you're bad enough when you're sober.
Peter All right, we'll take a cab.
Norma I'm not relying on a taxi to fetch me home, thankyouverymuch.
Peter Well what *are* we going to do?
Norma I don't care. I do—not—*care*.

She exits

Mrs Hinson (*of the television*) Hasn't he got lovely teeth? So natural. His mother was a permanent cripple you know.
Charles Really?
Mrs Hinson Mind you, I understand he's very good to her. You should get the *TV Times*, it gives you all the information. Oo-er . . . (*She leans forward to peer more closely at the television*) He's got the same shirt he had on last week.
Charles (*leaning forward*) Good Lord . . . I didn't notice that . . . did you notice that, Peter?
Peter (*through gritted teeth*) Ha-ha.
Mrs Hinson I wonder who does his washing?

Mrs Hinson and Charles look contentedly at the television. Despite himself, Peter also becomes absorbed in it as:

Hilary and Keith enter the kitchen. She is now dressed and carries a telephone on a lead which she plugs in and indicates for him to sit at the table

Hilary There we are.
Keith It's very good of you. (*He sits and dials*)
Hilary You didn't notice my husband, did you?
Keith Sorry?
Hilary Outside.
Keith Er . . .
Hilary Not to worry. He'll be out there somewhere, prowling around as usual. Probably looking for your ladder.
Keith Pardon?
Hilary Are you *awfully* good about the house? You seem to be.
Keith (*tapping the rest and dialling again*) I think I've got trouble in my loft.
Hilary I think David has. In fact I'm sure he has.

There is the sound of a door slamming off. On hearing it, Hilary shows her true concern

Oh God, I've gone too far this time—I've done something terrible to his mother.
Keith Pardon?

David enters from the hall. He carries two wine bottles in an off-licence bag and ignores Keith

David Where is she?
Hilary I killed her.

David (*it's possible*) You what?
Hilary I drowned her in a bucket of washing-up liquid.
Keith (*dialling again*) Evening.
David (*brusquely*) Good-evening.
Keith (*of the phone*) Won't be a jiffy.
David Oh I get it—she's packing her bag—you're a minicab-driver.
Keith No, I'm a freight officer at London Airport.
Hilary You'll find her in a crate on the landing.
Keith Typical—it's a recorded message.
David Hilary, for the last time, she's a pain in the neck but she's my mother!
Hilary She's watching her rotten *programme*.
David *Where?*
Hilary Over the road with the neighbours.
David The what?
Hilary The doctor and his wife. (*To Keith*) Just a minute, he's a doctor, why don't you have a word with him?
David Over the road with the neighbours?
Hilary He's a doctor, isn't he?
Keith Good idea.
Hilary (*to David*) I thought they'd have instant rapport. (*To Keith*) Do excuse me—I must turn the stair carpet—it's been down for almost a week.

She curtsies at David and exits to the hall

David Who *are* you?
Keith (*unplugging the phone*) We've got an emergency, she's having hysterics.
David Oh. (*He takes the phone*) You didn't notice my mother, did you?
Keith No. Sorry.

David exits to the hall with the phone and the bag

(*Following him*) Excuse me . . . you didn't notice my ladder?

Keith exits

Hilary enters the bedroom and sits miserably on the bed

David (*off; shouting*) Hilary? *Hilary!*

At the sound of David's voice, Hilary gets up and opens the wardrobe, examining the contents, as:

David enters, still holding the bag

What are you doing now?
Hilary I'm going to tart myself up, go out, and give myself to the first man who can prove he's an orphan.
David Are you seriously saying you took her across the road to watch *television*?
Hilary You could take her across the world and she'd watch television.

David It's all she's got.
Hilary Not—quite.
David (*moving to the door*) Thanks Hil, thanks very much. You've made a complete fool of me, haven't you?
Hilary Not a complete fool: you couldn't be a complete *anything*.

A moment

> *David exits to the landing*

> (*Instantly*) I didn't mean that, oh God, I didn't mean that. (*She slumps miserably on the bed*)

In the living-room, Charles, Peter and Mrs Hinson sit. Each pair of eyes glued to the television. Peter is trying to tear himself away as:

> *Susan enters the kitchen with the box of chocolates. She sits at the table and starts mechanically working her way through them as:*

Peter We'll get a cab there, give you a ring later, you'll pick us up.
Charles Go and see what she says.
Peter Right.

Peter exits from the living-room, keeping his eyes on the box as long as possible as:

Hilary exits from the bedroom as:

Keith enters the kitchen breathlessly

Katy is howling away upstairs

Keith Our bloke's away so I thought I'd try the one over the road, he's a doctor, waddaya think?
Susan (*mechanically*) She has a nervous breakdown, you run around looking for a doctor. I have a nervous breakdown, you build me a shelf to put my pills on.
Keith (*taking a chocolate*) I just thought I'd let you know.
Susan I am fat, I am ugly, and I don't care any more.
Keith Don't be daft, you're lovely, you'll spoil your dinner that's all. Did you tell them next door I'm a taxi-driver?
Susan I never speak to anyone. When I'm not looking after the kids or doing the shopping or the ironing or the washing-up, I'm looking out of the window. We haven't even got a phone. We've got a sidecar though.

There is a burst of thumping from upstairs

Keith I'll have to go. (*He moves to the door*)
Susan I shall be gone when you get back.
Keith Right.

He exits to the hall

Susan remains sitting as, in the living-room:

Mrs Hinson You see that one second from the left?

Charles Yes?

Mrs Hinson He fought back against incredible odds to become Scotland's Cavan O'Connor.

Charles (*sincerely*) Did he really, my word.

The front doorbell rings

Mrs Hinson Door!

Charles, deep in his viewing, doesn't respond. So that they both remain glued to the set as:

Susan exits from the kitchen to the hall with the box of chocolates

That'll be my David, come to see how I'm getting on.

Charles (*engrossed*) Jolly good.

Mrs Hinson Well aren't you going to let him in?

Charles Sorry?

Mrs Hinson I said I'm not the skivvy, you know. (*She levers herself from her chair and moves to the door*)

Peter enters cheerily

Peter Well that's it then, everybody's happy. There's someone at the door by the way.

Mrs Hinson That'll be my son, my David.

Peter He said something about an emergency.

Mrs Hinson He's a good boy, my David. I expect she's thrown herself out of the window again.

She makes to sit, contented, and Peter sees his hat just as she is about to sit on it again and snatches it out from under her. It has been squashed into a flat disc

Peter You've been sitting on my hat.

Norma enters brightly

Norma Has anyone phoned for a taxi? That's not him at the door, is it?

Peter (*showing her the hat*) She's been sitting on my hat.

Mrs Hinson I thought that cushion was a bit lumpy.

Charles (*still eyeing the box*) Well if it's an emergency shouldn't someone see what he wants?

Norma It's only a hat.

Peter It was an intrinsic part of my costume. Well that's it then, I'm not going. (*He sits*)

Norma Why not?

Peter (*waving the hat*) It's pointless now, isn't it?

Charles (*smugly*) It never had a point in the first place.

Mrs Hinson You can get some lovely hats in Marks. Mind you, if it's cheese you want you should try the British Home Stores.

Keith enters with a tentative little knock

Keith Excuse me.

Norma Yes, thankyousomuch, we know you're here.
Keith Sorry?
Norma Wait in the car, will you, we'll be five minutes.
Keith I wanted a quick word with the doctor.
Norma (*realizing*) Aren't you from across the road?
Keith That's right, the name's Bishop.
Mrs Hinson (*alerted*) Who's a doctor?
Norma I'm so sorry, I thought you were a taxi-driver.
Keith No, I'm a freight officer at London Airport.
Charles You see that one in the middle.
Peter What about him?
Charles His father was a gypsy.
Peter How d'you know?
Charles It was in the *TV Times*.
Norma How can we help you?

By now Keith too is watching the television

Keith We've got this friend arrived and she's having hysterics and we've phoned our own doctor, but he's not there he'll be yachting, so I wondered if you might be able to do something.
Norma What d'you think, Charles?
Mrs Hinson Is *he* the doctor? (*She is now all eyes for Charles: doctors are her gods*)
Charles What d'you mean by hysterics? (*He levers himself up*)

He shakes hands with Keith, both of them looking at the television

Charles Prentiss by the way, how d'you do.
Keith Keith Bishop, nice to meet you, she's shouting and screaming and crying and banging on the walls.
Mrs Hinson (*to Peter*) His previous was like that, you know, his Rosemary.
Norma Go on Charles, over you go.
Charles I can hardly go like this, can I?
Norma Well go and get changed.
Charles (*of Peter*) What about him?
Peter What d'you mean, what about me?
Charles You go.
Mrs Hinson (*eyes bulging*) Is he a doctor as well?
Charles More ethical anyway.
Norma Why is it?
Charles You know perfectly well—you don't treat your next-door neighbour unless it's an emergency.
Keith Well it is an emergency and she isn't your next-door neighbour, so do you mind? I mean, we are talking about human suffering. (*He sits down to get a better view of the television*)

David puts his head round the door and enters

David Excuse me . . . the door was open.

Norma Thankyousomuch, we'll be five minutes.

Keith (*standing, pointing*) Hang about, he's got a frock on.

Norma We were going out, you see.

Keith Ah. (*He sits again, satisfied, to resume his viewing*)

Norma (*to David*) Do you know Hampton Wick?

David Well I've got an aunt who lives in Twickenham.

Norma Just a minute, you're from over the road.

David (*generally, awkwardly*) Good-evening.

Norma Yes of course you are, I'm so sorry.

Mrs Hinson (*to Peter*) His best man was very nearly a doctor. Alan Longstaffe. He's a mobile chiropodist.

Norma (*to David*) Excuse me a moment. (*To Peter*) Actually I think Charles is absolutely right. You should go, Peter.

Peter But I'm an anaesthetist. It's years since I had a patient whose eyes are open.

Keith Look, if you're not going to help me I'll dial nine-nine-nine.

Norma Of course we're going to help you, but ethics do enter into it, you see: a doctor can get into all sorts of trouble just by trying to be helpful.

David (*to Mrs Hinson; brightly*) All set then, are we?

Mrs Hinson (*to Peter*) Do you know Doctor Stein?

Peter (*stiffly*) No.

Mrs Hinson He did my veins.

Norma (*opening the door*) Come along then, Peter.

Peter All right, all right, where's his bag?

Norma In the hall.

Peter (*to Keith*) Your mother sat on my hat.

He tosses the hat, like a frisbee, to Keith and exits

Keith gives the hat to Norma and bends to speak to Charles

Keith (*sarcastically*) Thank you Doctor, thank you very much indeed. (*He moves to the door*) What's he on about, my mother lives in Salford.

He limps out after Peter. As he does:

The bathroom door opens and Katy peers out. She is holding a hairbrush. She expected to find someone and is disappointed. She exits back into the bathroom, brushing her hair as:

Norma closes the door and beams at David

Norma Sorry about that, bit of an emergency. Now then, what can we do for you? I'm Mrs Prentiss by the way, Norma Prentiss, how do you do?

David Umm ... yes ... David Hinson, how d'you do ... I came to collect my mother actually and say thanks very much for having her.

Norma Not at all, we're delighted to meet you at last, aren't we Charles?

Charles (*eyes on the telly*) Sorry? Oh—yes—(*he levers himself up to shake hands briefly*)—how d'you do.

Mrs Hinson Doesn't he speak nice? I think doctors are wonderful.

Norma Offer Mr—er—a glass of sherry.

David Oh—well—ah.

Charles somewhat gracelessly pours a glass of sherry

Mrs Hinson His wife has just come out of hospital. She's supposed to be internal, but we could all say that, couldn't we?

David (*changing the subject quickly*) D'you play golf by any chance?

Charles Golf? Yes, I had a game once. It was like staring at a dead frog.

David Ah.

Charles hands him his drink

I was admiring your frock.

Norma My frock actually: we're going to a party.

David Ah! (*He takes a swig of sherry*) Off we go then, Mum, mustn't keep these good people waiting.

Mrs Hinson I am not going where I am not wanted.

David beams at Norma and Charles

Norma No hurry—we're waiting for a taxi. What time did you order it for, darling?

Charles Order what?

Norma The taxi.

Charles I didn't order anything. Ah good, the news. (*He sits, regarding the television*)

Norma Well didn't *anyone* order it?

Mrs Hinson Oh, we don't want to watch that rubbish.

And with no more ado, she gets up and changes channels. David knocks back his sherry. Charles stands, stunned, pointing at the television

Charles Excuse *me.*

Mrs Hinson No . . . there's enough misery in the world without having the news on television. All these meetings across the board the government keeps having—what do they want a board for, why can't they just sit down and discuss things? (*She settles back into her chair*)

Keith and Peter enter the bedroom. Peter is carrying a doctor's bag

Keith She's in the bathroom. I'll—er—I'll leave you to it then.

Keith exits to the landing

Peter makes to protest, then moves unwillingly to tap on the bathroom door

Katy (*off*) Who's that?

Peter I'm a doctor. Good-evening.

The bathroom door opens slightly and Katy puts her head out

Peter smiles amiably. Katy moves further out, appraising him and his white suit

Katy Are you *sure* you're a doctor?

Peter (*holding up the bag*) Anaesthetist actually.

Katy Oh.

She moves back towards the bathroom and Peter moves after her

Peter Well now young lady . . . what seems to be the problem?

They exit into the bathroom as:

In the living-room:

Norma (*massively impressed*) You work for *Sainsbury's*.
Mrs Hinson He's executive.
David Assistant chief buyer in the fruit and veg department.
Mrs Hinson My David was the man who introduced the pimento into Shepherd's Bush.
Norma Isn't that an amazing coincidence, Charles?
Charles Isn't what?
Norma *We* have a deep freeze and Mr—er—works for Sainsbury's.

The doorbell rings

Mrs Hinson (*immediately*) Door!

Norma exits obediently

David stares hopelessly into his empty glass

(*Pointing to the television set*) Oh it's her, I like her, don't you? She's always the same, so versatile. *She* . . . used to be a sergeant in the Salvation Army.

Charles decides he needs a large Scotch and pours a drink for himself and David as:

Keith limps into the kitchen from the hall

Keith Sue? Susie?

He limps out of the kitchen as:

Katy enters the bedroom from the bathroom and sits on the bed as Peter enters from the bathroom. He is drying his hands on a towel and is assuming his best bedside manner. He and Katy have taken an immediate fancy to each other

Peter Have you seen your own doctor?
Katy Only when I took the pills.
Peter (*tossing the towel back into the bathroom*) Which pills were these?
Katy The ones I tried to kill myself with.
Peter Uh . . . huh . . . (*He sits on the bed and puts a hand to her brow*) Well now young lady . . .
Katy Am I causing a tremendous amount of trouble?
Peter (*patting her hand*) No of course you're not.

The door is flung open and an agitated Keith enters, limping

Keith Where is she?
Katy (*clinging to Peter*) Don't shout at me, Keith—please.
Keith Where is she, she's gone.

Peter Now look here . . .
Katy I don't know where she went, honestly.
Keith Well she's not here and it's all because of *you*.

Katy runs, sobbing, into the bathroom

Peter I must ask you to leave this room.
Keith I pay your wages, mate—(*pointing threateningly*)—watchit!

He limps out of the bedroom, slamming the door

Bits of plaster waft gently down. Katy howls

Peter (*sighing*) Oh dear.

Peter exits into the bathroom

Norma enters the living-room followed by Hilary

Norma (*as they enter*) How are you finding the new house?
Hilary Oh we like it—(*she looks at David*)—I think.
Norma Of course the gardens are rather disappointing.
Hilary We've been admiring your tree.
Norma (*beaming*) I do love watching things *grow*. There are so few real pleasures in life nowadays, aren't there? (*Her face changes*) This is my husband Charles.
Hilary We've already met: hello again.
Norma Yes of course you have.
Charles Have we? Have we? (*He looks from one to the other, totally confused*)
Norma A glass of sherry, Mrs er——?
Hilary Hilary.

She hesitates, but sees that David is taking a swig from a glass

Thank you.
Norma We've been meaning to have you over for some time—do sit down.

She looks pointedly at Charles who pours a sherry for Hilary as she sits on the sofa. David moves to sit next to her. She takes his hand and they smile at each other, each silently apologizing for their argument. Mrs Hinson sits, mouth prune-like, increasingly irritated at being ignored as Norma hands round the nuts

Hilary (*almost taking one*) No thank you—I'm on a diet.
David (*quickly*) She's just come out of hospital, haven't you darling?
Norma Nothing serious, I hope?
Hilary They think I'm being poisoned.
Norma Oh dear: something in your system?
Hilary No: something in my family. (*She smiles at Mrs Hinson*)
Mrs Hinson Suffering isn't a patch on what it was in my day. Now we did suffer.

They all regard her

Norma We're going to a party but there seems to be some confusion about transport.

Mrs Hinson My hubbie was on the buses. He was spotless.

Charles (*to Hilary*) Is that lady your mother?

Hilary His mother. Isn't he lucky?

Charles But she turned off the *news*.

Mrs Hinson beckons Charles closer

Mrs Hinson She can't have children.

Charles Who?

Mrs Hinson You-know-who.

Hilary (*generally*) We don't want children. Sorry.

Mrs Hinson His previous could have children.

Charles Rosemary you mean.

David Oh my God.

Mrs Hinson Just a mo, I've got my snaps here somewhere.

Hilary (*icily*) Time for us to go, David.

Mrs Hinson Jump to it, boy—Madam has spoken.

David moves to where she is still searching her handbag, puts his hand over hers and tries to lever her from the chair

David (*brightly*) Off we go then . . . your programme's finished.

Norma No hurry—please—it's so nice to meet you at last.

Mrs Hinson pulls herself free of David, having trapped his hand in her bag. David rubs his hand

Mrs Hinson Course, he only sees them once a fortnight, poor little mites. Mind you, he's an exemplory father, exemplory. When he gets the chance. (*And she's already levering herself from the chair*) Now then . . . who's ready for a nice cup of tea?

She makes her way to the door and David slumps into the chair and Hilary glowers at him

You want to put a drop of paraffin in the water next time you do those windows. They come up like new.

Mrs Hinson exits

Norma turns to look at the "windows"

Norma They are new.

Mrs Hinson enters the kitchen, shakes the kettle to check its contents and switches it on as:

Norma beams and then turns to Charles, still holding her false smile, and all four speak quickly and sotto voce

Norma Will you please go and find Peter?

Charles What's the point? He said he wasn't coming anyway.

Hilary Are you just going to sit there?

David Who brought her here in the first place?
Hilary That's right, go on, change the subject.

David downs his drink and stands. He moves determinedly to the door

David (*generally*) I'm sorry. I am, I am very sorry.

He exits from the living-room and enters the kitchen as:

Mrs Hinson is opening a drawer where she finds a natty little apron which she puts on

Norma (*offering the nuts*) Do have a nut—oh no, you're dieting.
Hilary (*seizing the bowl*) Not any more.
Norma Excuse me.

Hilary ploughs through the nuts as Norma switches off the television

Charles, you're beginning to make me angry again. (*She flutters her fan wildly, pacing*)

In the kitchen:

Mrs Hinson I will not go . . . where I am not wanted.

She opens a cupboard. David closes it again and she opens another one

David We don't *know* these people.
Mrs Hinson Well you should do, he's a doctor. And between you and me, by the way she dresses I wouldn't be surprised if she wasn't a Justice of the Peace—like that Mrs McCracken who kept the fish shop. Why do you think I'm being so nice to them? I'm trying to do you a bit of good, my son. Now then . . . let's see if I can find you a nice biscuit . . .

She opens another cupboard, but David shuts it again

David I do not want a biscuit—I do not want a cup of tea—I want you out of here—out!

He glares at her then exits from the kitchen as:

In the living-room:

Charles (*standing suddenly*) Right! We're going.
Norma Then will you please telephone for a taxi.
Charles I shall drive.
Norma But you won't be able to get drunk which means you'll be totally unmanageable.
Charles Norma—I am determined to be the life and soul. (*He downs his Scotch*)
Norma (*to Hilary*) God help us.

David enters the living-room as:

Mrs Hinson puts biscuits on a plate and exits from the kitchen to the hall with the plate

David moves straight to lean over Hilary, who ignores him, looking straight ahead and chewing in the nuts

David I've told her . . . all right . . . I've *told* her . . . (*He straightens up, slaps his hands together cheerily*) We'll be off then.
Charles So soon?

Mrs Hinson enters the living-room. She gives the plate to David and turns straight to Charles

Mrs Hinson Ah there you are, Doctor . . . I was wondering if you could give me a prescription while I'm here.
Charles What for?
Mrs Hinson Oh I don't mind, really—how about something for my nerves?
Charles Who *are* you?
Hilary (*cheerily*) My mother-in-law. Isn't she sweet?
Mrs Hinson I get very breathless when I run.
Charles So do I.
Mrs Hinson You don't think a prescription might help?
Charles Trust in Mother Nature—Mother Nature knows best, believe me.

Charles exits

Mrs Hinson (*undeterred; to Norma*) He's not giving much away, is he? I suppose he's private.

The front doorbell rings

Door!

Norma exits obediently

David (*moving instantly to Mrs Hinson*) Out!
Mrs Hinson I am not going where I am not wanted—and eat your biscuits.
Hilary Do you really think they want you here?
Mrs Hinson Who brought me here in the first place?
David Leave her.
Hilary How can we leave her, they're going out.
David *Leave* her.

Norma enters the living-room with Keith whose limp has increased along with his concern

Norma Mr—er—can't seem to find his wife.
Keith You haven't seen her, have you?
David Me?
Keith When you were looking for my ladder.

Charles enters, now wearing his wig

Charles Before we go any further, I am well aware that Marlene Dietrich did not wear a moustache.
Mrs Hinson She wore a top hat though, definitely. (*Suddenly*) Oo-er, the kettle.

Mrs Hinson exits from the living-room and enters the kitchen, where she bustles around as:

David gives the plate to Norma and makes to pour himself a sherry, but instead pours a Scotch

Norma Mr—er—can't seem to find his wife.

Charles I'm sure you'll find her here somewhere—have you looked under the sofa?

Keith Pardon?

Norma (*hissing*) Offer him a drink.

Charles (*hissing back*) We are going out.

Norma Don't be so—morbid.

Charles (*to Keith*) I understand you'd like a drink before you go.

Keith (*slumping on the sofa, next to Hilary*) I think I could do with a whisky.

Charles So could I. (*He takes the bottle from David*) Any left, is there? (*He pours drinks*)

Keith (*to Hilary*) I think she's gone.

Hilary (*flatly*) Oh dear. Have a nut.

She offers him the nuts. He searches the debris for a whole one as David knocks back his drink and holds out his glass to Charles

David Very kind of you.

Charles gives him the bottle, gritting his teeth

Charles (*to Norma*) I need to know which way to point the car: will you please show me the invitation.

Norma Certainly. (*To Hilary*) Oh dear, you've finished the nuts. Do have a biscuit.

She hands the plate of biscuits to Hilary and exits

Keith I do. I think she's finally gone and left me and it's all my fault.

David No no no . . . it's *my* fault . . . isn't that right, darling? Whatever it is, whatever goes wrong, it's my fault . . . my . . . fault . . .

He beams around, clearly under the influence, knocks back his Scotch and exits, taking the empty glass as:

Charles and Keith drink and Hilary savages a biscuit as:

David enters the kitchen and stands, his back to the audience as;

Mrs Hinson bustles around as:

Peter and Katy enter the bedroom from the bathroom. They sit, feet up on the bed

Peter It can't all be your fault, surely?

Katy Gareth says I'm too compliant and not only that I dress all wrong.

Peter How did you meet?

Katy I was having a sort of ding-dong with the scrum-half and I suppose I
was sort of passed along the line. Gareth plays on the wing you see:
there was no-one outside him so he sort of did the decent thing.

In the living room:

Keith There's no-one she can turn to, you see. Not since we moved. No-
where she can get things off her chest.

*He absently holds up his glass for a refill and Charles resentfully takes the
glass and replenishes it as, in the kitchen:*

Mrs Hinson Your Rosemary wouldn't have spoken to me like that . . .
David What are you talking about? You hated Rosemary. You've hated
every woman who's got within ten yards of me.
Mrs Hinson You're my son. If a mother can't make her son the occasional
rice pudding . . .
David I *hate* your rice pudding. I hate your custard, I hate your seedcake,
I hate all your food—it's rotten, it always has been—I don't know how
the old man survived it so long.
Mrs Hinson Don't you dare bring your poor dear father into this . . .

Norma enters the kitchen and looks into a drawer, preoccupied

David Poor dear father? Poor dear father? You nagged the life out of
him. Why d'you think he spent hour after hour in that stupid bloody
tool-shed of his? He couldn't stand the sight of you. D'you know—the
only time I saw him smile, really smile, was when he knew he was
dying. Death, the blessed release. God help me for saying it but it's
true, it's true.

*Norma has found what she was looking for—the invitation—and she exits
from the kitchen*

A moment

Mrs Hinson I see.
David I mean look at you now. Making tea in someone else's kitchen—
they don't want you to make tea, they want you to go home.
Mrs Hinson I only try to do my best for people, for all the thanks I get.
David Mum . . . you're my mother and I love you but I don't like you. I
want to . . . but I don't *like* you. (*He sits, his back to her*)
Mrs Hinson Don't worry, son. Don't worry, David. You've said your
piece. Still. I shall be dead soon and then I'll be out of your way, won't
I? (*She kisses him briefly on top of the head*) Cheer up—I'll make you a
nice cup of tea whether you like it or not. (*She bustles back to the kettle*)

*David heaves a great sigh, puts his head in his hands and remains sitting thus
as, in the bedroom:*

Katy How long have you been divorced?
Peter Oh . . . years.
Katy What went wrong?

Peter Well . . . most men end up marrying their mothers. I ended up marrying my father.

He waits for her to get the joke. She doesn't. So he becomes very serious again

Anyway . . . *(he sighs)* . . . you don't want to listen to my stupid little problems.

Katy I do. Promise.

She takes his hand as:

Norma enters the living-room brightly and moves straight to lean over the sitting Keith and Hilary with a bright but patently insincere:

Norma No hurry—*do* finish your drink.

Hilary Is my husband still with his mother?

Norma Yes, I believe he is.

Hilary takes another vicious bite of biscuit as Norma gives the card to Charles

Two minutes and we're off.

Charles All of us?

Norma makes to go out, but can't resist leaning over Hilary

Norma Do let me know if you'd like a tin of corned beef or something.

Norma exits

Charles glares at the invitation

Hilary I lost nearly six pounds last week. Six pounds.

Keith I know how you feel: I've just lost a fifteen-millimetre ring spanner.

Norma enters the kitchen where David still sits, hands to head, as Mrs Hinson bustles around

Norma Ah, there you are, Mr Hilary—your wife is looking for you.

He looks at her, then is suddenly on his feet

David Then who am I . . . who am *I* . . . to delay?

He grins wildly, drunkenly, at Norma and exits to the hall

Mrs Hinson You see what I mean? Now then . . . who takes sugar and who abstains?

Norma *(the gracious lady of the house)* They've changed their minds, I'm afraid: no-one wants anything.

Mrs Hinson Well that's charming, I must say. I'm not the skivvy you know. And incidentally, I'm not one to criticize, never have been, but how you find anything in this place I'll never know.

Norma Well that's what I wanted to talk to you about, actually.

Mrs Hinson What's that, dear?

Norma I'm just about to advertise for some domestic help. I was wondering if you knew of anyone who might be interested.

She remains, her back to the audience and Mrs Hinson remains, hands on hips, as though listening as, in the living-room:

Keith (*glumly*) I thought moving out of the flat into a nice new house would make her, you know, happy. By the way, your over-flow is over-flowing.

Suddenly Charles is looking closer at the invitation

Charles Ahhh!

Keith New house, new friends——

Charles (*stabbing a finger at the invitation*) Ahhhh! (*He moves to the door*)

David enters

Charles thrusts the Scotch bottle into David's hands and exits

Keith —nice big garden for the kids . . . nice big garage for the bike . . . I thought she'd be happy.

David (*leaning between them*) Good-night all.

Hilary Where are you going?

David I shall either commit suicide or go jogging. As ever—I am totally—totally—undecided.

David exits from the living-room as:

Charles enters the kitchen. He brandishes the invitation at Norma and his accent increasingly reveals his Welsh origins as he speaks

Charles It's not this week . . . it's next week . . . you've got the wrong date . . . the wrong *date*.

Norma Oh dear.

Charles Oh dear? Oh *dear*? *Look* at me. Well . . . you wanted a party, you shall have a party . . . (*He moves to the door. As he exits*) It's party time! Party time!

Charles exits

Mrs Hinson moves smartly to the kitchen door to shout after him

Mrs Hinson Get a grip on yourself, you're a medical man! (*She resumes busying around, muttering away to herself*)

Norma exits from the kitchen as:

In the bedroom, Peter is hopelessly trying to get a word in edgewise

Katy They'll want to see his bank statements and everything which could prove rather tricky in view of that nasty business with the tax people last year. Do *you* have tax problems?

Before Peter can answer, Susan enters the bedroom from the landing, wearing a topcoat

Immediately Katy pulls away from Peter, leaving him stranded on his back

Susan I'm so sorry, I didn't realize you had a visitor.
Katy This is Susan, she lives here—Sue, this is . . .
Susan Excuse me, I'm looking for my chocolates.
Peter Chocolates?
Susan I left them last time I came up. Perhaps you could sort them out for me when you're not too busy.

She smiles and exits

Katy Oh God, she gets so *emotional*.

She exits quickly after Susan

Peter Chocolates? I haven't seen any chocolates . . . (*He gets off the bed and bends to look under it. And we see that the seat of his beautiful white trousers is covered in melting circles of chocolate. He finds the squashed box of chocolates on the bed*) Eureka!

He exits from the bedroom holding the box triumphantly before him as:

Charles enters the living-room. He has a manic gleam in his eye and is full of amazing bonhomie

Charles Have another drink. (*He almost snatches the glass from the sitting*

Keith and tops it up and fixes one for himself)

Hilary (*standing*) I think I ought to find my husband.
Charles Good idea—bring him over—tell him we're making a night of it.
Hilary (*uncertainly*) Oh—well—thank you. (*To Keith*) If I should—um—see your wife . . .
Charles Bring *her*. Bring who you like. Invite the entire neighbourhood.

Hilary exits, still uncertain

Charles hands Keith his glass and stands, looming over him as:

Mrs Hinson exits from the kitchen to the garage

Charles We've never really spoken, have we?
Keith Pardon?
Charles I say we've never really spoken. (*He sits next to Keith*) What do you think about living on this estate? I rather like estates, don't you? I even like the word. Estate. Interesting word, estate, don't you agree? (*During this, he stretches an arm along the sofa, behind Keith*)
Keith 'S all right. (*He suddenly becomes aware of the arm behind him*) Actually . . . I'm thinking of forming a residents' association. I'll be needing the likes of you if you're willing.
Charles How do you mean—the likes of me?
Keith Well . . . a doctor, figure of the establishment and all that rubbish. Mind you, if you do join the committee and we have to go down the town hall, I'd be grateful if you'd wear a pair of trousers.

Norma enters the living-room and hovers somewhat nervously

Charles (*withdrawing his arm*) Might I ask if you're a Communist?

Norma Charles can't even afford to be a Socialist, can you, darling?
Keith (*brandishing the yachting magazine*) He can afford to buy a yacht
though. (*He knocks back his drink and stands*) Cheerio.

But Charles is on his feet and moves so that they are face to face

Charles While we're on the subject of transport, might I ask you to park
your car a little less flamboyantly: I happen to be a doctor and liable to
be called out at a moment's notice, day or night.
Keith *Eh?*
Norma (*quickly*) We also notice you have a motor cycle.
Keith You're not saying there's anything wrong with my bike, are you?
Norma No—we admire it—often.
Keith That bike is an antique.
Norma Then it must be quite valuable.
Keith Why does it always come down to money with you people?
Charles *What* people?
Keith (*pointing*) It's people like you who lobbied against the sidecar.
Charles (*moving closer*) Now look here—*chutney* . . .
Norma Careful darling, your roots are showing.
Keith How come you get a telephone and I don't?
Charles Did you *ask* for one?
Norma Why don't you bring your charming wife over for a drink?
Charles *I'll* tell why we've got a telephone . . .

The front doorbell rings

Norma That's all right darling—I'll go—you stay here and finish your
sentence.

She exits

Keith And I'll tell you something else.
Charles What?
Keith You can stop sneering at my garden.
Charles Oh it's a garden, is it?
Keith I've got some really great ideas for that garden, really great.
Charles Why not start with the fence?
Keith No pond—and a real tree.
Charles That tree as you call it is my wife's pride and joy.
Keith And that's another thing.
Charles What is!
Keith Stop peering at my wife!
Charles I haven't *seen* your wife!
Keith Neither have I!
Charles And whose fault is that!
Keith It's the fault of people like you, putting on frocks and peering at her
out of the window—that's who!

Norma enters the living-room with Susan

Norma This is Mrs—er—she's looking for her husband.

Keith (*immediately surprised and pleased to see Susan*) Hello. Where've you been?

Charles is left in impotent rage, as Norma beckons him to leave the others on their own, and they exit

Susan and Keith are each trying to play it cool

Susan You know she's got a bloke up there, do you?

Keith He's a doctor.

Susan (*sceptically*) Oh yes?

Keith He's a friend of this one—where've you been?

Susan For a walk. You weren't the only one, you know. They all had her down that club. Every one of them. They call her The British Open.

Keith Don't start all that again, Sue—please—not now.

Susan You and I are finished. When the children come back I'm taking them to my mother's.

Keith They're already at your mother's.

A moment. She doesn't know whether to laugh or cry and he starts to kiss her

Susan If we're going out, I'd better wash my face.

She takes his hand and leads him to the door

Keith Actually love . . . I think we've been invited to a party . . .

They exit as:

Mrs Hinson enters the kitchen from the garage holding a bundle which she unfolds, holding it up, and we see that it is Peter's trousers. As she thrusts them into the bowl in the sink:

Peter enters the kitchen from the garage, wearing everything except his trousers and hungrily chewing on an apple. He perches on the edge of the table

Mrs Hinson If ever you're over Lewisham way, pop in and have a proper meal. My David will give you the address.

Peter Mmmm . . . yes . . . thanks.

Mrs Hinson Yes, he's a funny boy my David. If you ask me he's on the verge—well, I'm not surprised, living with you-know-who. I was wondering, Doctor—as a medical man—if you could have a word with him.

Peter Ah—well now—not really my province you see—I'm an anaesthetist.

Mrs Hinson Oh I think he could do with a good night's sleep. (*She scrubs away happily*)

Peter exits to the hall chewing the apple as:

Keith and Susan enter the bedroom, each holding a glass

Keith There.

Susan (*looking round*) But it's exactly the same as ours.

Keith But it isn't ours, is it? (*He turns off the light*)

Susan What are you doing?
Keith It's a party, isn't it? What did we used to do at parties?

He takes the glass from her, sets down both glasses, lifts her up, lies her on the bed and starts to kiss her as:

> *Mrs Hinson exits from the kitchen to the hall with the rolled-up bundle of trousers*

> *Peter enters the bedroom, turning on the light. He is still without trousers and has a cigar in his mouth*

Peter Oops, sorry, won't be a jiff.

Keith and Susan watch, frozen in their embrace, as he opens a wardrobe and takes out a pair of Charles's trousers. He moves to the door

> *(Confidentially, to Keith)* I've just had a word with your mother. There's a chap I know in Harley Street—have to go private of course—anyway —let me know what you think—*(he puts a finger to lips)*—sorry.

He turns off the light and exits, tip-toeing as:

> *Charles—minus the wig—enters the living-room with Katy. She's been giving him the treatment and he's well-flattered. Each holds a glass which Charles replenishes*

Katy Poor Gareth. I only hope he's happy. Apparently I've got to apply for maintenance and so on. The solicitor says I can nail him to the mast, whatever that means, I've never really understood legal terminology. It's at times like this a woman feels so helpless. Do *you* play rugby?
Charles Not any more I'm afraid. Used to, of course.
Katy Yes I thought so: you've got the body. *(She squeezes his biceps)*

Norma enters the living-room

Charles The thing being, of course, I've always managed to keep myself in shape.
Norma The thing being, of course, he was that shape to start with.

She smiles sweetly at Katy who does her twirling around bit

Katy I think this is a super room . . . really super.

Norma glares at Charles and thrusts her glass at him for a refill

Oh, by the way, there's someone in your pond.
Norma I beg your pardon?
Katy He sort of fell in and came up waving a sort of stick.

All three look out of the "window" as:

> *David enters the kitchen. From the knees down he is soaking wet and is clutching the remnants of Norma's tree which still has part of the stake attached to it. He stares at it hopelessly and exits into the garage*

Norma Well he's not there now.

Charles Too dark to see anyway.
Katy No, he sort of ran away.
Norma (*sceptically*) Really?

In the bedroom, Susan turns on the bedside light. She and Keith are sitting on the bed

Susan Are you sure they won't mind?
Keith Course they won't.

Susan reaches down and takes up a telephone from beside the bed. As she starts to dial, Keith gets up and limps to the door

Won't be a jiffy . . . What's he on about, Harley Street?

He exits, closing the door, as:

Peter enters the living-room. He is now wearing Charles' trousers which are too full and too short

Peter Right then, who's for a dance?
Norma What a lovely idea.
Katy Super.

They both turn to him but he advances towards Charles, arms outstretched

Charles (*grimly*) Lay one finger on me and I shall sue.

In the bedroom:

Susan (*on the phone*) Hello Mum, it's me, how are they?

Hilary enters the kitchen, wearing a simple but glamorous frock

Hilary David . . .? Where are you, we've been invited to a party . . .

She exits through the open door into the garage

Norma Charles, see if you can find your record.
Katy (*to Peter*) Actually . . . I've got some cassettes in the back of my car.
Peter Oh really?

She holds out a hand, he takes it, and they exit hand in hand, Peter being led willingly to the slaughter

Susan (*on the phone*) Say that again, darling. . . . Dad-dee. . . . Yes. . . . Daddy. . . . Stay there, I'll go and get him, you can say it to him. Keith, he's just said his first word . . .

She opens the bedroom door, just as Keith, cigar in mouth, is about to climb the step-ladder

Keith Hello love—I said I'd have a quick look at his over-flow.

Susan slumps

Keith climbs the steps and goes out of sight

(*Off*) Actually, he's not a bad bloke, that doctor. He used to have the old Brough Superior you know.

Susan returns to take up the telephone, leaving the bedroom door open as:

Hilary and David enter the kitchen from the garage

Hilary Where did you put that wine?

David takes a bottle of wine out of the fridge

I'm sorry about your mother.
David No. It's my fault.
Hilary I don't know what gets into me.
David (*kissing her lightly*) I'll take her home tomorrow and that's the last you'll need see of her till Christmas—and that's a promise.
Hilary She's not that bad. I suppose.

David gently shunts her towards the door

David Well, anyway, let's go and see what she's up to.
Hilary (*at the door*) Why are your trousers wet?
David What trousers?

They exit to the hall as:

Mrs Hinson enters the living-room

Charles has found his elderly record and is about to put it on the turntable

Mrs Hinson (*to Norma*) Have you discussed it with your hubby?
Charles Discussed what?
Norma (*nervously*) Mrs—er—is going to help me with the cleaning.
Charles (*horrified*) Mrs Er is *what*?
Mrs Hinson Mondays, Wednesdays and Fridays would suit me best. Give me a chance to keep an eye on my David.

Charles stares as she turns on the television and then moves to him

I know what I wanted to ask you, Doctor—a woman I know is going in for an eastereggtomy. Now I ask you: is this strictly necessary?

The front doorbell rings

Door!

Norma exits quickly

Mrs Hinson settles down to watch television. Charles resists the urge to break his record over her head

Black-out

CURTAIN

FURNITURE AND PROPERTY LIST

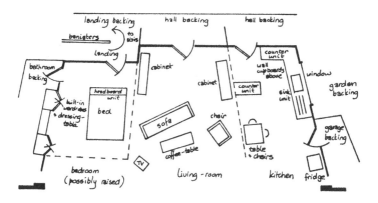

ACT I

On stage: **Living-room:**
Sofa. *On it:* cushions. Under one: copy of *The Guardian*
Easy chair
Coffee-table. *On it:* ashtray, yachting magazine
2 polished hardwood cabinets. *In one:* bottle of sherry, bottle of
   Scotch, glasses. *On other:* record player
Television
Vacuum cleaner (practical) and duster (for **Mrs Hinson**)

Bedroom:
Double bed. *On it:* sheet, pillows, duvet
Headboard unit. *On it:* bedside light, cigarettes, matches, ashtray
Built-in wardrobes and dressing-table unit. *In wardrobes:* dressing-
   gown, 2 dresses. *On dressing-table:* mirror, hairbrush

Landing:
Unpacked tea-chest (optional)
Step-ladder (to be set outside bedroom door prior to page 29)

Kitchen:
Table. *On it:* notepad, pencil, steel tape measure, car keys, handbag
   (for **Norma**)
2 chairs
Sink unit (practical). *In it:* washing-up bowl. *By it:* tea-towel. *In cupboard underneath:* tin of Swarfega

Counter units. *On top:* toaster on serviette, electric kettle, teapot. *In drawers:* ball of string, meat skewer, cutlery. *In one cupboard underneath:* large tin of biscuits
Wall cupboards. *In them:* tins of food/glasses/crockery/one empty.
Fridge. *In it:* dish of pears and jug of custard
Waste-bin (full)

Off stage: Potted plant arrangement **(David)**
Sink plunger **(Charles)**
Tray with 2 mugs of tea, newspaper **(Keith)**
Miniature tree staked in pot, handbag, car keys **(Norma)**
Plastic basket full of washing and pegs **(David)**
Weekend suitcase **(David)**
Notepad and pencil **(Norma)**
Carburettor **(Keith)**
Filthy tea-towel **(Keith)**
Hot-water bottle, duster **(Mrs Hinson)**
Towel **(Susan)**
Tea-towel, hot plate loaded with stodgy food **(Mrs Hinson)**
Wide-brimmed black hat **(Peter)**
Bottle of sherry **(Peter)**

Personal: **David:** glasses, handkerchief
Mrs Hinson: handkerchief, handbag containing bottle of pills, small photograph album
Norma: rollers and plastic hood
Charles: pipe, wrist-watch
Keith: coins
Charles: cigarette holder, evening bag containing pipe and tobacco pouch
Peter: wrist-watch

ACT II

Strike: Dessert bowl from kitchen

Set: **Living-room:**
Record in cabinet

Bedroom:
Skirt, top, pair of trousers in wardrobe
Bottle of pills in dressing-table drawer
Telephone on floor beside bed
Conceal squashed box of chocolates on bed for **Peter** to find on page 71

Landing:
Cigar for **Keith**

Kitchen:
Bottle of wine in fridge
In drawer: apron, invitation card

Off stage: **David's** sweater, sponge (Mrs Hinson)
          Yachting magazine (Charles)
          Cigarettes, matches, box of chocolates in paper bag (Susan)
          Plate of stodgy food (Hilary)
          Remains of plant arrangement (Hilary)
          Black shawl and **Peter's** hat (Norma)
          Bowl of pistachio nuts (Norma)
          Telephone and lead (Hilary)
          Bag containing 2 bottles of wine (David)
          Box of chocolates (Susan)
          Hairbrush (Katy)
          Doctor's bag (Peter)
          Towel (Peter)
          Pair of white trousers (Mrs Hinson)
          Apple (Peter)
          Glass of drink (Keith)
          Glass of drink (Susan)
          Glass (Charles)
          Glass (Katy)
          Remnants of tree and stake (David)

LIGHTING PLOT

Practical fittings required: television flicker effect, bedside light, pendant in bedroom

Interior. A living-room, a bedroom, a kitchen. The same scene throughout

ACT I   Summer afternoon to early evening

To open: General daylight effect in all areas except bedroom, which should be dimly lit as though curtains are drawn

ACT II   Summer evening

To open: As at end of Act I

EFFECTS PLOT

ACT I

ACT II

PRINTED IN GREAT BRITAIN BY
LATIMER TREND & CO. LTD, PLYMOUTH

Lightning Source UK Ltd.
Milton Keynes UK
UKOW06f1053120116

266248UK00013B/192/P